THE BUSES AND
TRAMS OF PA

BRIAN PATTON

ISBN: 978-1-900515-06-1

Published by: DTS Publishing, PO Box 105, Croydon
www.dtspublishing.co.uk

Printed by: Ian Allan Printing Limited

British Library Cataloguing in Publication Data. A catalogue record for this book is available from the British Library.

Abbreviations used in the text

APTR	Association Professionelle des Transports Routiers
AMTUIR	Association pour le Musée des Transports Urbains, Interurbains et Ruraux.
CGO	Compagnie Générale des Omnibus
CGPT	Compagnie Générale Parisienne des Tramways
CMP	Compagnie du Chemin de Fer Métropolitian de Paris
RATP	Régie autonome des Transports Parisiens
RER	Réseau Express Régional
STCRP	Société des Transports en commun de la Région Parisienne
SOMUA	Société d'Outillage Mécanique et d'Usinage d'Artillerie
STIF	Syndicat des Transports en Ile-de-France
STP	Syndicat des Transports Parisiens
TPDS	Tramways de Paris et du Département de la Seine
UTPUR	Union des Transports Publiques Urbains et Régionaux

COVER COLOURS reflect the flag of Paris which is blue and red with blue to the mast.

FRONT COVER: Renault TN 4 F 3012 awaits its next turn of duty at Pigalle in April 1968. *(Author)*

FRONTISPIECE: The only double-deck buses operated by RATP were twenty-six Berliet PCMRE as illustrated by an unidentified example arriving at l'Opera terminus of line 53 in September 1975. *(G. W. Morant)*

BACK COVER: Modern trams, Citadis 412 and TSF2 203, at Belvedere on Line T2 in June 2003. *(Author)*

CONTENTS

Champs d'Elysées 15th August 1970. *(Julian Osborne)*

Introduction

The genesis of this book goes back a long way, to 20th July 1955 to be precise. On that day our school party, who were staying in Saint-Mandé, was due to go to Versailles. I had, however, noticed that there was an exhibition of Jules Verne in what was then the colonial museum at Porte Dorée and, being a great enthusiast for that writer's works, I asked if I might be allowed to go to that exhibition instead. After some deliberation, permission was given, on the strict understanding that I was not to go on the Métro, in which I had shown a great interest. Being grateful for the privilege, I kept my promise, but, once the exhibition had been visited, saw no harm in spending an hour watching and photographing the buses at the busy junction, where the Petit Ceinture (PC) bus service intersected many other lines and most of the buses were those with old-style rear platforms. It was fascinating and I immediately added an interest in the buses to that in the rail system. That interest has endured to the present.

From a British perspective, the road transport system in Paris has always played second fiddle to the Métro. Visitors probably find the latter easier to use, particularly if they do not speak French, since the routes are clearly displayed and it is easy to form a mental map of the system fairly quickly. The former system of stage fares also made a road journey more complicated than one underground. Transport enthusiasts too have favoured the Métro, partly for its inherent fascination, partly because it has for most of its life been a very good advertisement for underground railed transport. It is, however, a pity that surface transport has been thus neglected. Bus routes cover much of Paris and a bus journey can give a visitor a view of many of the city's sights, much more economically than a ride on one of the tourist services. There is also more chance of talking with a fellow passenger, rather than when underground, where for most of the day the trains are virtually mobile reading rooms, enlivened only by the occasional busker.

This present book was conceived as a way of righting the historical balance and of giving an insight into one of the world's most highly developed bus networks. The Paris bus has a long and distinguished history and the network has had to cope with the effect of two world wars, the second also involving occupation by enemy forces. Under the auspices of the RATP, there has since the 1970s been steady progress and in many respects the bus system can now act as a model for that in other countries. It has of course been shaped by political decisions at different times, but it has to be said that its managers have been left to do the job with much less interference from politicians than has been the case in Britain. RATP will very soon celebrate the 60th anniversary of beginning operation and in that time its structure has changed little.

This book aims to give both a historical perspective of the road services and also to provide an up-to-date picture of the vehicles and facilities involved in that service. Basically it deals only with the services of RATP, with a very brief look at sightseeing services. The number of buses in service within the Ile-de-France area is very much greater than that of the RATP alone, but the suburban operations could require a book to themselves to give a proper idea of their scope and within this publication there is simply not room enough for that. Where street names have been changed, the present name is given in brackets after the original name.

Recently the tram has made a very impressive comeback in Paris and the next few years will see considerable expansion of the network, with the introduction also of rubber-tyred vehicles on the Translohr system. It seemed right, therefore, to include the trams. The Montmartre funicular is also covered in a short section – most tourists see it, many are very glad to use it and it would be a pity to neglect it.

The information given is correct as of 16th October 2008, but in a developing system, changes will inevitably occur within a short space of time. The details given on extensions are correct according to present information, but there may be changes before they are completed. Whatever the final outcome, however, it can be said with certainty that the attention given to planning of the entire transport system and the monies spent on its development will ensure that Paris retains its place as a world capital with a first-class transport network, a place that visitors and those living in less fortunate countries can only look on with envy.

It would not have been possible to have produced this book, particularly with regard to the illustrations, without the unstinting help of Thierry Assa, Vice-President of AMTUIR, who has patiently downloaded, from his own collection, many of the illustrations of older vehicles, as well as supplying much useful information to supplement that in printed sources. I am also grateful to M Phillippe Benoît (now retired) of the Centre de Documentation in the Maison de la RATP and to his colleagues who have been most helpful over a series of visits. In the United Kingdom I appreciate the additional photographs provided by Peter Shearman, Ron Phillips, Mike Davis, Julian Osborne and Brian Rowney; thanks also to Malcolm Chase for his help in providing appropriate examples from his collection of Paris bus, tram and funicular tickets.

BRIAN PATTON
FOULDEN
BERWICKSHIRE
SCOTLAND.

14TH MARCH 2009

Buses of Paris

Paris, of all the world's capitals, was the first to inaugurate what could reasonably be called a stage carriage service and, although that did not last for very long, it has had the longest continuous period of bus service. Services began in 1828 and have continued ever since, with only a brief break between 1914 and 1916.

The early service was devised by Blaise Pascal, a mathematician and philosopher of the 17th century. In 1661, by which date the population of Paris numbered about 400,000, he obtained backing from several aristocratic patrons to set up a service of carriages in the streets of the city, plying on fixed regular routes and available without pre-booking to passengers of the classes defined in the ordinance governing the operation of the service. The plan was put to the royal council and on 19th January 1662 Louis XIV signed a decree of letters patent confirming the creation of a "Compagnie des Carrosses à Cinq Sols" (Five sous carriage company)*. Later decrees were issued governing the operation of individual routes. These were quite lengthy documents and were exhibited on placards at various cross-roads., laying down the exact route to be followed and specifying that the carriages had to operate whether or not there were passengers. They had to run to a fixed timetable, but there were no fixed stopping places. It seems that when the first route came into operation, some individuals had prevented other passengers joining en route, effectively using the vehicle as a private hire cab, and the decree for the second route stated firmly that this could be done only if eight fares were paid, the capacity of the vehicles being eight. Later carriages had a capacity of eleven. The carriages were also numbered in a rather curious way, by a number of fleurs-de-lys painted on the front beside the driver. Anyone who had a complaint had only to note the number thus painted and report this to the office to gain recompense. (It is not clear where these offices were.) The vehicles carried the arms of Paris on the side and the drivers wore blue coats. The services were intended solely for the use of the bourgeois and the fare of five sols (about 2½d/1p) effectively prevented anyone not of the middle class from using them, but just in case any of the lower orders had ideas above their station, the ordinance expressly forbade soldiers, artisans, workmen, pages and servants in livery from boarding a carriage.

It seems to have been the intention that the entire city would be served by a network of routes, which would all offer good connections one with another, but no transfer fares were offered. In the event five services were operated, as follows:

Porte St-Antoine – Luxembourg, rue St-Antoine – St-Roch, rue Montmartre – Luxembourg, rue Neuve St-Paul – St-Germain-des-Près, rue de Poitou – Luxembourg.

The enterprise was launched with a fanfare, according to Pascal's sister who wrote of *"un éclat et une pompe merveilleuse"* (a good deal of pomp and ceremony). The inauguration took place on a Saturday, (probably 21st January 1662) at 7am, three of the seven carriages being stationed at the Porte de Saint-Antoine and four at Luxembourg, where there were assembled a large crowd of notables, including four Commissioners of the Châtelet in their ceremonial robes and ten or twelve of the city archers. When all was ready, the commissioners proclaimed the inauguration of the service and exhorted the passengers to be strict about not admitting any of the lower orders. If any of the latter offered them the slightest insult, they would, by command of the King, be strictly punished. Presumably Louis had already anticipated that public transport could be a social leveller. Having given the drivers their coats, they then set the first carriage off on its way. The second left a quarter of an hour later and so on, until all were in service. For that day, all carried a guard, but all passed off peacefully and these had little to do.

The horses used would seem not to have been of the highest class, since the poet Loret referred to them as *"des chevaux non rosses"* (horses which could not be called steeds), but despite this, the system was initially successful and for some time attracted a considerable traffic. Unfortunately Pascal himself died on 19th August 1662. However, average speed must have been low and the people allowed to use the carriages would also have been those who would have aspired to own their own carriage, when funds permitted. The number of passengers declined and the last carriage ran in 1677. It was to be just over 150 years before anyone else would try to follow the example of Pascal and his backers. Parisiens had to make do with cabs, of which there were 2,542 in 1819.

---

*The "sol" or "sou" was the lowest denomination of pre-decimal currency in France and, in very rough terms, was equal to an English halfpenny at that time.

The Local Government background

Before looking at the history of the bus services, an explanation of the structure of local government in the city and surrounding area may be helpful to those who are not familiar with these.

When permanent bus services were started in 1828, the layout of the city of Paris was still basically that of the mediaeval city, consisting approximately of the area lying within what are now lines 2 and 6 of the Métro. In 1790 this had been divided into 12 arrondissements (administrative districts). In 1860 the city's area was extended to include the land lying between that and the fortifications which had been erected between 1841 and 1846 and thus it attained its present extent, with the addition of a small amount of land on the site of these fortifications when they were dismantled after the first world war. The original arrondissements were modified and the additional area was divided into eight new arrondissements, the two areas together being referred to as *"Paris intra-muros"* (Paris within the walls). Names such as Porte d'Orléans still commemorate the gates in these fortifications and these places often form a terminus of both the Métro and many bus lines. In the past, they also acted as customs points, where zealous officers collected the "octroi", a tax paid on goods entering Paris. This had implications for buses and later trams running into the city from outer suburbs, which had to wait while the officers went about their duties; they were not above lifting the skirts of respectable housewives who had been shopping for cheaper goods in the suburbs, to check on any concealed items. Paris was not, however, a totally independent municipality, since in many matters it came under the authority of the Département of the Seine, by which it was completely surrounded. Beyond the city area lay the remainder of this Département, sub-divided into many local authority units, such as Aubervilliers, each with its own municipality and mayor, the latter having much more executive authority than an English mayor or Scottish provost. The Mairie (office of the mayor) is very often the terminus of local bus lines, being, for example, shown on destination indicators as "Mairie du 18ème" (mayor's office of the 18th arrondissement). Beyond that area lay the Département of Seine-et-Oise. By legislation passed in 1964 the Département of the Seine was split up, with Paris now becoming a département in its own right and the remainder becoming the Départements of Seine – Saint-Denis (north and north-east), Hauts-de-Seine (north-west, west and south-west) and Val-de-Marne (south-east and south). At the same time, the Département of Seine-et-Oise was divided into the three Départments of Val-de-Oise (north), Yvelines (west and south-west) and Essonne (south). The Département of Seine-et-Marne, which lay to the east of Seine-et-Oise, was not altered and has retained its former boundaries until the present day. To-day all this area forms the Région of Ile-de-France, the inhabitants of which are known as Franciliens.

Although the city had a municipal council during this period (with a few breaks due to war), it also came under the control of the Prefect of the Seine and the Prefect of Police, both of whom were appointed by central government. In some respects Paris had less individual authority than an English county borough and from 1794 until 1977 it did not have an elected mayor, the first occupant of the present post being Jacques Chirac, who held office until his election as President of the Republic in 1995. The dual authority led to a number of conflicts, of which that relating to the building and ownership of the Métro was the one to have most influence on transport, but surface transport, in particular the tramways, was also affected at times. From the time of the arrival of the main line railways in the early 1840s, there were also disputes between these and the municipal authorities, as the railway companies, with some support from central government, sought to penetrate nearer to the city centre than the termini constructed at that time ; their efforts were, with two exceptions**, unsuccessful and these termini are still in use, albeit much rebuilt.

The urban development of the Paris area had also differed from that of London in another respect. Paris has not at any time been surrounded by other towns, such as Croydon, East and West Ham or Kingston, which are important urban centres in their own right and which in due course would grow inwards to meet the expanding city. The only exception to this was the royal town of Versailles to the south-west, with Saint-Germain to the west and Saint-Denis to the north also showing signs of urban growth, though on a small scale, the latter having only 15,000 inhabitants in 1851, when the population of the city had reached the 1.5 million mark. To the north, east and south of the city there were, until about 1880, only villages. Partly because of rebuilding of the city centre in the mid-19th century, the better

---

**The lines from Gare d'Austerlitz to Quay d'Orsay and Champ de Mars to Invalides, both opened in 1900.

off did not take flight to the suburbs, as was the case in elsewhere, but continued to live within Paris itself and the resident population of the inner city was, and to an extent still is, a much higher proportion of the total population of the urban area than would be the case in Britain. The population of Paris reached the figure of 2.9 million in 1914 and this figure remained more or less constant until about 1960, since when it has declined to 2.1 million in 1999.

With industrial development, the suburburban area began to grow from 1880 but even in 1914 still accounted for only 25% of the population of the urban area. Only after 1918 was there rapid, and very often chaotic, growth of the suburban areas and by 1939 over two million people lived in these. The trend continued after 1945, now going along with government policy of reducing the importance of Paris in favour of the rest of the country. Development was greatest in the outer suburbs (*la banlieue de la grande couronne*) and many of the inhabitants who moved out to those areas had to face long journeys to and from work in Paris. The tedium of the suburban commuter's existence was summed up in 1968 by the writer Pierre Béarn in the phrase *"Métro, boulot, bistro, mégots, dodo, zéro"* (Métro, work, food, fag-ends, bed, zilch), which during the upheaval of 1968 was abbreviated on many a wall to *"Métro, boulot, dodo"*. By 1962 the number of people commuting daily into Paris from the suburbs was 900,000.

At the same time, inter-suburban commuting was increasing at a rapid rate and, as neither rail nor bus services catered for this, most of it was by private car. Car ownership increased in the outer suburbs at a much faster rate than it did within the city itself and car commuting followed this trend. Between 1965 and 1991, car trips within Paris increased only from 25% of all journeys to 32%, whereas in the outer suburbs it grew from 46% to 80%. This was not good news for the bus. Matters were made worse in 1966 by the introduction of the five-day week, which saw Saturday traffic fall by almost 50% over the RATP network.

The Fifth Republic, under General de Gaulle, was set up in 1958 and in the 1960s it reversed the policy of (relatively) neglecting Paris in favour of the provinces. The Law of 2nd August 1961 created the District de la Région de Paris, its first president being Paul Delouvrier, a close colleague of President de Gaulle. In 1965 this body produced the first Schéma directeur d'aménagement et d'urbansime de la Région Parisienne (General plan for the restructuring and urban development of the Paris region). This plan proposed the construction of five new towns such as Saint-Quentin-en-Yvelines which, though primarily connected with the development of the Résau Express Régional (RER), also significantly expanded the operation of the road services of the RATP. Much more attention was now given to public transport, although in the 1960s this invariably meant rail transport. Credits were made available for both public transport and road building, although the latter always had the lion's share. Nonetheless the urban transport benefited from these, to the tune of 2.13 million francs annually between 1971 and 1975.

The Development of Bus Services

It should be noted that bus services in Paris were until about 1987 rigidly divided into city and suburban operations and in less defined form, this division still operates. City services were relatively short by London standards and ran only within the city of Paris itself. They had central area termini, such as Saint-Lazare and the suburban terminus was very often at the location of one of the former city gates. Even lines which went beyond these penetrated no more than a few hundred metres into the suburban communities. Suburban services, which began only after 1922, were very often centred around local railway stations or, after the Métro was extended into the suburbs from 1934 onwards, at one of its stations. While this arrangement was logical for journeys to and from the central area and for very local traffic, it did not help passengers who wished to travel from one suburb to another. There was no equivalent to services such as London's 2 or 122, which ran either from a suburb, through the central area and out to another suburb, or from one suburb through various others to another suburban terminus. Services generally finished at 20.30 and what were termed *"Services de nuit"* (night services) ran on a reduced frequency from then until about 23.30. As in London, there was not until recent years a comprehensive network of services running during the night. While services were and are generally less frequent on Sundays, and some lines do not run at all, the network was and is basically that of week-day services and there were no special Sunday or holiday services. Paris buses have always run 365 (or 366) days a year.

The inauguration of the first bus service was due to the efforts of one Stanislas Baudry, of Nantes. As a colonel in the armies of Napoléon 1, he found himself redundant after Waterloo and, being of a mechanical turn of mind, invested in a mill, powered by a steam engine which, co-incidentally, could heat water to a temperature comfortable for bathing. To use this water, he set up a bath house at some distance from the centre of Nantes and, to encourage custom, put on a service of carriages from and to the city. As these had spare capacity, he allowed the public to use them, even if they were not patronising his baths. In the event, the carriages proved to be much more popular than the baths and, flushed with the success of this service, Baudry decided to try the idea in Paris. By an order of 30th January 1828 the Prefect of Police authorised the operation of one hundred buses on ten lines and on 11th April 1828 services began. Five started from Bastille and served Bercy, Place du Trône (Pl de la Nation), Place du Carrousel, La Villette and Porte St Martin. Two had a terminus at Pl de la Madeleine and ran to Barrière des Bonshommes (Quai Kennedy) and to Rue de Lancry. Two others began at Quai Conti and served la Monnaie and Jardin du Roi (Jardin des Plantes) while the tenth ran from Place de Carrousel to Barrière des Ternes. Buses stopped on demand but drivers were forbidden to stop at cross roads, on bridges, at cab stands and, after 6pm, outside theatres. The frequency was supposed to be quarter-hourly but traffic congestion made it difficult to keep to this schedule. Initially the flat fare was 25 centimes, but this was soon raised to 30. The network met with great approval from the Parisians and by 15th October, the Entreprise Générale des Omnibus had carried 2,630,624 passengers.

Unfortunately this approval also brought competition and as early as May 1828 another company, the Dames Blanches (White Ladies) had appeared on the scene. By the end of 1829, there were ten in all. Paris was awash with buses, trading under a variety of names and painted in a rainbow hue of colours. The Algériennes and Constantines commemorated the war which was currently being waged in Algeria, the Dames Blanches (White Ladies) ran from a terminus at the old Opera (Square Louvois) and the Ecossaises (Scottish Ladies) ran buses whose livery was made up of many different colours, though, unlike those which later ran in Glasgow, they could not really claim to be tartan. A company called "Les Tricycles" developed a design of vehicle with only one wheel at the front, operators of this design having to pay less tax than on conventional buses. Naturally the city authorities took a dim view of the idea, but in any case these buses proved impractical and did not last long in service. In all there were 21 companies and competition was so ruthless that it was all too much for Baudry, who also had financial problems following an unsuccessful property speculation in Passy. He committed suicide by plunging from the Quai de Jemappes, where one of his depots was possibly situated, into the Canal Saint-Martin in 1830, having also taken the precaution of shooting himself in the head as he jumped. It was also almost too much for his company, but it was taken over by one of the shareholders, Aristide Moreau-Chaslon, and, under his management, the Entreprise Générale des Omnibus remained the most important. Many of the competitors did not last very long. The Dames Blanches, for example, which ran only 15 vehicles, was declared bankrupt in 1840, was rescued and in 1850 amalgamated with the Dames Françaises to form the Dames Réunies. Only eleven companies were still running in 1853, using a total of 360 vehicles. As was to be expected, the operators concentrated on the profitable lines in the city centre and showed no enthusiasm for the less densely-populated suburbs. Only one line served the north-east of the city and only two ventured into the south-west and, despite all the efforts of various governments, this remained the case until 1914.

The urban structure began to change with the establishment of the second Napoléonic empire in 1852. One of the first acts of Napoléon III was to appoint as Prefect of the Seine one G-E Haussmann, with the remit of improving the city in several ways. The clearance of many slums and the laying out of a number of new and wide boulevards (which helped to improve the speed of the buses) were to be Haussmann's main legacy to the city, but he was also interested in transport and strongly believed that the current chaotic pattern of bus operation was not the best way to serve his new city. When the Prefect of Police, one P-M Piétri, acting with the full approval of the Emperor, proposed in January 1854 the amalgamation of the various companies into a single operation, his suggestion fell on receptive ears and on 22nd February 1854 the Compagnie Générale des Omnibus (CGO) was created by imperial decree, to come into operation on 1st March. It was given a thirty-year monopoly, to run from 1st June 1854, within Paris, (and in the suburban communities of Vincennes and Courbevoie) in return for an annual payment to the city authorities and a guarantee that it would also serve the less lucrative routes. The rolling stock was to revert to the city on the expiry of the concession and the Prefect of Police had the right to impose a scheme of modernisation on the company, in the event of technical developments. By this date there were also separate companies working in the suburbs. Moreau-Chaslon became chairman of the board of the combined Paris undertaking and his brother, Jean-Louis Moreau, was put in charge of the horses. The creation of the CGO came just in time to help the buses to cope with the five and a half million visitors who came to the city in the summer of 1855 to visit the first of its international exhibitions. In that year, 40 million passengers were carried. By 1st January 1856 25 lines were being operated within the city, these being distinguished by letters of the alphabet, from A to Z with the exception of W. The lines were also distinguished by colour bands on the sides of the vehicles and at night by double colour lights, this scheme being so arranged that no two services with the same colour combination ran on the same street. The Madeleine-Bastille line E had a yellow colour band and at night two red lights.

When the area of the city was greatly enlarged on 1st January 1860, with the creation of eight new arrondissements (13th to 20th), the sphere of operation of the CGO was extended to cover the newly-annexed areas and some immediately beyond, with twelve new lines. This development required the agreement of a new concession between the city and the CGO, signed on 18th June 1860. Given that the latter had been making considerable profits since 1855, the municipal authorities were now less inclined to be generous and fairly strict terms were laid down, in addition to those carried over from the earlier concession. This concession was to last for fifty years. The city was to receive a half share of the profits when the dividends went above 8% and the road tax was increased. The CGO had been adding to its profits by dealing in the property market and this was now to be limited, in favour of the further modernisation of the fleet. The growth in the number of lines required new indications to be used and, as they had now run out of single letters, the CGO began to use double letter indications. Thus the new line from Passy to the Bourse was designated AB. With the expansion of the city area and the general growth in traffic, 74 million passengers were now carried annually and in the year of the next international exhibition, 1867, this figure had grown to 122 million. Although they grumbled about overcrowding and the speed of the buses, Parisians had by now taken this form of transport to their hearts. When the exiled Prince Imperial, son of Napoléon III, was asked by a friend which sight of Paris he would most like to see again, he mentioned not some famous monument, but the sight of the Grenelle omnibus turning out of the rue du Bac.

There were now 21 lines in operation in Paris, worked by a fleet of 753 vehicles, requiring a stud of over 7,000 horses. The busiest line, in 1867, (line E, Madeleine-Bastille) required 45 buses and thus 450 horses, to provide a three-minute service, carrying 647 passengers per bus per day, or almost 30,000 in total. Due to the rough ride on cobbled streets, it was not uncommon for a baby to be born in a bus and line E held the record for the greatest number of babies. All the vehicles then in service could carry 24 passengers. Although the new suburban lines were less profitable than the former core network, business and dividends remained satisfactory until 1873, apart from a slight downturn during the Franco-Prussian war of 1870-71 (which brought about the end of the Second Empire) and the subsequent trouble of the Commune. During the siege of Paris in the winter of 1870/71, buses were used as ambulances to convey wounded defenders of the city from the fortifications to the Val-de-Grâce hospital and for this purpose they were fitted with a light awning over the upper deck.

The CGO was, as far as its horses were concerned, a model operator. At its maximum, its stud comprised 16,500 animals, since each bus required the daily service of five teams (ten horses), as the distance each team travelled was in the region of 16km. The teams always consisted of the same two horses, save in cases of illness, and, as far as possible, horses were paired with another of the same disposition. They always had the same driver, and conductor. The daily ration, in 1867, was valued at 2.59Fr (about 3/

- in sterling). In contrast to contemporary practice in Britain, the CGO did not dock the tails of their horses, taking the view that a horse needed its tail to cope with flies. Trace horses were provided to assist on steep hills, of which there were 31 in the city. Each horse had two weeks holiday per year, during which it would be sent to the country to perform light work on a farm. A vet visited each depot once per week and inspected the animals; any which seemed to be unwell were immediately sent to the hospital and the box which they had occupied was disinfected. All this cost the CGO a great deal of money, but in return it obtained years of good work from its stud and some horses were still giving excellent service when they had reached the age of 15. They commanded a good price when they were finally sold off. Generally the horses appear to have been happy with their work and they were noted for their docility and intelligence, attributes which greatly helped the smooth running of the system. However, one day, somewhere in the 9th arrondissement, a horse, which had clearly had enough, managed to slip its harness and jumped over a bridge to its death before the crew could catch it. There was considerable public debate about the type of horse which was best suited to bus work – the French were not as reticent as the Victorians in Britain about such

ABOVE: The general appearance of horse buses in Paris is well seen in this busy scene on the Boulevard Montmartre about 1906, with a two-horse bus on the left. Most of the traffic is still horse-powered, although a motor taxi can be seen further to the left. The bus on the right displays the yellow and black colour scheme. Although it is clearly a sunny day, the drivers of the various vehicles are well wrapped-up. Traffic is flowing smoothly and, for the moment, under the large gas lamp, the gendarme with the baton is content to watch it pass. *(Author's collection)*

BELOW: A view looking east along the rue Saint-Lazare from the station. A fairly orderly queue seems to have formed in the carriageway prior to boarding the bus on the right, with its typical cramped platform and stair. Other pedestrians walk happily across the street, apparently oblivious of the stream of horse-drawn traffic. This card was posted in June 1907. *(Author's collection)*

Scènes Parisiennes. — Agent réglant la circulation des Voitures et des Piétons.

ABOVE: Although the CGO generally looked after its horses very well, it has to be said that the example on the right appears rather dejected! A gendarme tries to exert some control of the traffic in front of the Opéra and on the left, competition for the buses is provided by the horse-drawn taximeter cab, with its aloof lady passenger. *(Author's collection)*

BELOW: The first departure of the morning on line E, probably at Madeleine. Horses and staff alike look rather cold and the man on the right seems to be wearing a muffler, something which at a later date would not have been allowed! *(Author's collection)*

matters – and it seemed that, while animals which had not been neutered were stronger and more vigorous, they were also temperamental and more susceptible to illness, while geldings were calmer and coped better with frequent stops. At a later date, however, the latter were used much less and in 1867 there were only about 700-800, of a total stud of 9,656 animals . Mares were not to be trusted, as they were too capricious. Horses came from Normandy, Brittany and Le Perche.

The crews seem to have been fairly well treated too. In 1867 wages began at 4Fr per day and rose to 5Fr after three years service. These figures would have been equivalent to 8/- and 10/- in contemporary £ sterling. The working day was long, beginning at 06.45, and the last bus did not run into the depot until after midnight. Crews had to buy their own uniforms, but these were sold to them by the Company at a reasonable rate, a complete outfit costing, in 1867, about 100 francs, or about £12. The uniform was considered to be quite glamorous in the mid-19th century. It was royal blue in colour, with silver buttons and was worn with a black tie. Free medical care was provided and there were insurance and pension schemes. Supervision by inspectors was strict but, in view of the good terms of employment, the CGO generally had little difficulty filling vacancies and fraud was kept to a minimum. However, an attempt to organise a trade union in 1891 resulted in the dismissal of the men concerned and this led to an acrimonious strike. Unions were finally recognised early in the 20th century. Bonuses were also awarded for honesty in handing in lost property, of which there was a considerable amount, to a total value of FR95,000 in 1867.

There had been one tram line operating in Paris from 1858, but, to protect the interests of the CGO, it had been limited in its area of operation and had posed no real threat to the buses. However, in 1873 the creation of a network of tramways was set in motion by a decree signed by President MacMahon on 9 August. (France was now a republic.) This placed the Département de la Seine in overall charge and this authority, contrary to practice in London and Berlin, subsequently agreed that the CGO should have a monopoly of tramway operation within Paris, subject to the payment of an annual fee of FR6,000 per kilometre. Unlike either London or Berlin, Paris enjoyed a fair measure of co-ordination of bus and tram services. However, as with the two other cities, some streets in the central area were barred to trams and the buses retained a monopoly on these. This system was profitable for the CGO which, in years up to 1900, paid a dividend of about 6% to its shareholders.

With the exception of the Chemins de Fer de l'Ouest, which operated out of the Gares Saint-Lazare, Montparnasse and (from 1900) Invalides, the main line railway companies had not developed their suburban services by 1900. However, the Petite Ceinture railway, which encircled the pre-1860 area of the city, had an important passenger service, carrying 39 million passengers in 1900. Some of these companies, such as the Ouest, also operated buses to connect their termini with the city centre

The same year, 1900, saw the opening of the first sections of the Paris Métro, run by the Compagnie du Chemin de Fer Métropolitain de Paris (CMP). As this was built under the auspices of the City, the CGO was more than a little annoyed that its monopoly was now being assailed by a competitor from the same authority. With stations just below street level and spaced fairly closely – within Paris these are generally about 440m apart – the Métro was a much more serious competitor to the buses than were the tube lines in London. By 1914 it covered, in outline, most of the inner urban area.

Meanwhile the horse buses and the variety of trams soldiered on, but from 1901 onwards, they no longer produced any profits and no dividends were declared from that year until after 1910. Working expenses more or less equalled receipts and the various payments which had to be made to the authorities resulted in a substantial loss on operations. Although the number of passengers

189   PARIS · PREMIÈRES VOITURES DU MATIN

carried on all forms of transport in the city (excluding suburban railways), rose form 486.5 million in 1901 to 682.1 million in 1906, the CGO's traffic figures remained virtually static. The Company then spent more on a legal action against the City, claiming that the latter was in breach of its agreement, but it lost this. In 1910 the concessions of all the tramway operating companies, not only the CGO, were re-negotiated and a level playing field was created in matters such as fares, conditions of work and control of services. All were now to last until 1950. All companies were required to modernise their fleets and the CGO lost no time in ending operation of horse-buses and trams and also the weird and wonderful collection of mechanically-propelled vehicles which ran on the tramway network. The last horse-bus ran on 11th January 1913 on line L. Villette – Saint-Sulpice. Parisians in their thousands turned out to watch its passing and the horse was suitably commemorated by a placard decorated with a laurel wreath surrounding a large photograph of a horse and the single word "Merci". The event was captured on film and, although the horses must have had some difficulty with the overcrowded vehicle, it was a much more suitable commemoration than the passing of the last horse bus in London some months earlier. The last horse-tram ran in April of the same year.

Although the CMP was not included in the above settlement, the new arrangements worked well and there was a great increase in passenger numbers of 114% on the bus system.

Unfortunately the outbreak of war in August 1914 completely upset this happy state of affairs. All buses were requisitioned on 2nd August and used for military duties or to carry provisions to the army. None returned to civilian service. It was not until 1916 that, with permission from the Ministry of War and using women conductors, the CGO was again able to operate bus services in Paris. The war also caused severe inflation and, once peace had returned in 1918, the trade unions began to agitate for increases in wages and improved conditions. The CMP bore the brunt of this unrest, but as its terms and conditions of employment had been used as a point of reference by those in other companies, they were similarly affected. Not only were prices and wages rising at a rapid rate, well ahead of the increases in fares which were reluctantly granted, but a raft of new social legislation – the eight hour day, three weeks annual leave and retirement at 55 – all imposed a financial burden on public service operators. In the case of the CGO, this amounted to an annual increase of 50 million francs (c£5million). All these considerations led to a proposal in December 1918 that the Département of the Seine should take over all the private companies and operate the network as a public service. Nothing was done at the time, but, despite further increases in fares in 1919 and 1920, financial stability was not restored and at the end of the former year, the CGO was able to serve only 25 bus lines, against the 43 which had been operating in August 1914. Public control seemed to be the only solution and in September 1920 a decree created a new system, to come into operation on 1st January 1921. All bus and tram companies would be acquired by the state and passed to the Département for administration and all surface transport would be amalgamated into one authority, the Société des transports en commun de la Région Parisienne (STCRP). André Mariage of the CGO became head of the new authority. Once again the CMP was not involved in this settlement. The new authority inherited a bus network of 258km, serving 41 lines with 734 vehicles. At the same time, a first step towards co-ordination was taken with the creation of a consultative committee for Paris transport, made up of representatives of the Départments of Seine and Seine et Oise, the city of Paris and the national government. Neither the main line railways – not, with the exception of the Chemins de fer de l'Ouest, as yet nationalised – nor the Métro were represented on either the STCRP or the committee. The latter did not propose anything very useful though it did begin to take a firm anti-tram stance, believing that the trams were a source of congestion in the streets. However, the new organisation allowed the return of financial stability, largely thanks to a loan of 400 million francs taken out by the STCRP. For the bus system, the acquisition of a large number of new vehicles was the most obvious sign of this. By 1925 72 lines were in operation, including many in the rapidly-developing suburbs, where the first new line had been placed in service in 1922. The bus fleet had grown to 2,370 vehicles. Bus passenger numbers were rising at a satisfactory rate. Unfortunately, despite this growth, profitability remained elusive and competition from the Métro was growing as road traffic and thus congestion increased. In 1929 it was agreed that the Métro should be allowed

ABOVE: Several bus and tram lines had their terminus at Gare de l'Est, as seen in this view taken about 1912. On the left, the double-deck trailer of a tram-trailer set disappears into the rue de Strasbourg (rue du 8 Mai 1945), while in the centre of the picture one of the prototype Schneider PB2 single-deck motorbuses awaits its next departure on line B to Trocadéro. The entrance to the Métro, with the ornamental stone balustrade, is nearer the camera. Between the bus and tram, a couple dressed in the height of fashion cross the road; he wears a bowler and his friend an extremely narrow "hobble" skirt and picture hat. *(Author's collection)*

BELOW: The same terminus on 9th April 2008, seen from a point slightly further from the station. Agora L 1712 (on left) and Heuliez gas-powered 8056 await departure. *(Author)*

PARIS — Gare de l'Est

197. PARIS – La Gare St-Lazare
Côté de la Cour de Rome – A. P.
The St Lazare Terminus (by the Rue de Rome)

ABOVE: An interesting picture of the transition of the CGO. It shows Saint-Lazare and must have been taken in 1911. On the left is one of the P2 double-deckers, then in their last months of operation. A new PB2 occupies centre stage, while one of the last horse buses can be seen to the right, beside the bus station. *(AMTUIR, collection Assa)*

to extend beyond the municipal area into the inner suburbs, the first such extension (on Line 1 from Porte de Vincennes to Château de Vincennes) opening in 1934, and these extensions abstracted some passengers from the buses. Labour troubles also cropped up in the decade and there were strikes on the bus network in 1925 and 1928, of which the former was successful in bringing about improved conditions for staff and thus further damaging the finances of the STCRP.

The replacement of the tramways, first seriously proposed in 1927, was at the heart of a new contract between the operator and the Départment, signed in 1930, and thereafter implemented with great enthusiasm. By 1937 the tram had disappeared from the city's streets (a suburban line remained in operation until the next year) and in consequence the bus fleet had increased to 4,067 vehicles. In 1934, the bus service PC also replaced the antiquated steam trains of the Petite Ceinture railway line. Total passenger numbers were, however, falling, more or less in proportion to the growth of those using the Métro.

The election in 1936 of the Popular Front government, with Léon Blum as prime minister, completely upset the financial balance of the STCRP. Among the new social measures passed by this government

were the introduction of the 40hour week and paid holidays, coupled with a general increase in wages. To keep the system going, it was necessary to take on 3,600 new employees, plus several hundred temporary workers. As the Départment was unwilling to do anything constructive to restore equilibrium, the national government, now centre-right under Chautemps and with Paul Reynaud as Finance Minister, stepped in and enforced a fare increase of 33%, to be implemented in three stages. Passenger numbers immediately fell by anything between 15% and 40%, depending on the nature of the line concerned. Several lines were withdrawn and others saw a reduction in their frequency. By a decree of 12th November 1938, the government also set up a Paris Transport Committee, which first met on 12th January 1939 and included representatives of the French National Railway (SNCF) – now operator of the main line railways – and of the Métro. It was intended to be a transitional body and, probably because of the attitude of some right-wing deputies on whose votes the government depended, nothing had been achieved on the ground by the outbreak of war in September of that year.

All bus services ceased on 12th June 1940, when the vehicles were requisitioned to move troops to the front. They resumed on 31 August, but on a very limited scale, as there were only 500 buses available, against 3,500 in 1939. When matters had become somewhat more settled, the government, which had removed to Vichy (France was now under occupation) turned its attention to the matter of Paris transport. Given that parliament had been sent on indefinite holiday, that the trade unions had been stripped of their powers and that public opinion had few chances to make itself heard, it was possible for the government to proceed more or less as it wished to and by a "law" of 26th June 1941, it decreed that the STCRP and the CMP should merge with effect from 1st January 1942, the combined system being placed under the management of the latter. A division to run the surface network was created under the directorship of Pierre Mariage, son of André, but, as there was little to run anyway and as there was no attempt to align the methods and cultures of the two constituents, very little co-ordination was actually achieved. The only practical result of the merger was a harmonisation of fares, based on the practice of the STCRP. Details are given in the section on fares and tickets. In 1943 the first trolleybuses appeared on the streets. In general terms, the Vichy government was unenthusiastic about Paris, though as the city was under German control from June 1940 to August 1944, there was not a lot that they could have done about it anyway. By 1944 the number of buses in service had declined to 275.

Naturally it was difficult to maintain services under conditions of war and occupation, quite apart from the shortages of materials and fuel. The central workshops were in part requisitioned by the Germans and were used to repair army vehicles. This was known to the Allies and in consequence they suffered severe damage in an air raid on the night of 20/21 April 1944, when the smaller workshop at Saint-Ouen was also damaged. The new administration was also favourable to the Vichy government and implemented its decrees with regard to Jewish passengers and communist employees zealously. The Resistance had many supporters within the transport system and acts of sabotage occurred from 1941 onwards. A general strike was called on 12th August 1944 and what services there still were ran for the last time on 17 August. Many drivers had also refused to drive buses to the front in Normandy during the Allied advance. Deportations continued up to the

BELOW: Replacing such a large tramway system over a few years was a mammoth task and sometimes conversions were phased, the inner section of a line being converted first and the suburban part some months or even years later. In this view, at Cimetière de Pantin in 1935 a class L tram on line 51 awaits passengers who have been brought from the city by what is probably a Renault TN 6 C2 bus. The section of this line from République to Porte de Pantin was converted on 20th November 1933. The next stage, onwards to Cimetière de Pantin, followed on 16th July 1934 and the last, from there to Drancy, took place on 14th April 1936. *(AMTUIR, collection Assa)*

PANTIN — Route des Petits-Ponts - Entrée du Cimetière parisien E. M.

end and many Jews were saved at the last minute by Resistance members in the road service who removed the carburettors from the fleet of buses which was to take them to the railway yards for onward transport.... It was certainly not a happy time and the feelings which were then aroused played a large part in the post-war difficulties of reconstruction and co-ordination.

Once services resumed, form 25th August onwards, control of the system was provisionally given to the Prefect of the Seine and on 3rd January 1945 Paul Martin, head of the combined undertaking, and Pierre Mariage, were removed from their posts, on the grounds that they had been too co-operative with the Vichy régime. At the same time, a Provisional Administration of the Métro was set up under René Clauson, a former Inspector of Roads and Bridges. This provisional system was in fact to last for almost four years. As the cold war started and the post-liberation political consensus gradually broke down, it became more and more difficult to legislate for the future structure of Paris transport. However, on 21st March 1948 a law was finally passed setting up the Régie Autonome des Transports Parisiens (RATP) and on New Year's Day 1949 this authority assumed control of both the road services and the Métro. The new authority was run by a board of 28 members, of whom five represented the French government and five were chosen by the Minister of Transport. As far as the bus fleet was concerned, there was little outward sign of the change.

Unfortunately, as originally created, the RATP was bound to balance its budget and also to provide a public service maintaining the various concessionary fares which were in operation in 1949, such as those for large families. From 1952 onwards, this dual mission became virtually impossible, especially as successive governments refused to allow any increase in fares between August 1951 and January 1958. The organisation had to be baled out by the local and national authorities, to prevent a complete cessation of service, but the system was clearly unsatisfactory and little was available for investment. Most of what there was went to the road services, since they had been so badly affected by the war, and the Métro was largely left to make do as best it could. By 1958, 40 new lines had been placed in service and the number of buses risen to 2,900.

Also set up by the law of 21st March 1948 was the Office Régional des Transports Parisiens (ORTP), with members representing both the French government and the local authorities. Intended to have a co-ordinating role, it achieved little in its first years, but it did produce a plan in 1950 which led to the creation of new services both within Paris and in the inner suburbs and to cope with these, the bus fleet was expanded considerably. In 1951 RATP staff produced a second plan providing for the replacement of all pre-war buses but as there was no money for this, nothing was actually done. By and large, the ORTP was a distinctly damp squib.

While the administrative structure was being thus reorganised, a great deal of hard work by the maintenance staff had made it possible to restart some suburban services in the autumn of 1944 and in November lines PC and 26 resumed service within the city. By October 1946 there were 96 lines in service, 31 within Paris. These required 1500 buses and it was hoped to add another 500 in the course of 1947. By 1950 services were back to the pre-war level. A record number of passengers was carried in 1948 ((898 million) and thereafter numbers settled down to around 800 million, a level at which they remained for

most of the 1950s. Within the city, services were now designated by numbers, rather than the former letters.

The 1950s were not a happy period in the history of Paris transport. Many of the vehicles were clearly out-moded, the lack of finance for new projects made it difficult to recruit engineers and administrators of the necessary calibre and the operating staff felt neglected and saw a reduction in their status compared to that of staff in other public enterprises.

The new government of the Fifth Republic, set up in the autumn of 1958, tackled the problem in a series of decrees issued between January 1959 and November 1962. The financial basis of the contract between the government and the RATP was completely altered and the ORTP was replaced by the Syndicat des Transports Parisiens, with greatly extended powers. But perhaps the most significant point of the changes was to show to the travelling public that, at last, the central government was taking urban transport seriously and had recognised that the system in Paris had to be considerably improved from its current state. The appointment of Pierre Weil as Director-General of the RATP in 1963 also brought about significant changes in the organisation. Weil's background was in main line railway operation and, as he had had no connexion with either the STCRP or the CMP, he came to the RATP free of any taint of what had happened during or just after the war. However, he was mainly involved in the gigantic tasks of effecting improvements to the Métro and of creating the RER and he did not personally contribute much to the road services.

Unfortunately just at the time when central government policy changed, other factors combined to bring about a sharp decline in the number of passengers using the bus system. With a good deal of backing from Georges Pompidou, who was prime minister from 1962 to 1969 and then president until his death in 1974, the number of private cars on the road increased rapidly. In the Paris conurbation, there had been 500,000 cars in 1950 ; this figure had increased to 1.2 million by 1960 and to 2.36 million by 1970. But this increase was not evenly spread across the region. Within the city, the number of cars per household rose only from .39 in 1962 to .57 in 1991, whereas in the outer suburbs it rose from .50 to 1.25. Having invested in a car, people naturally wanted to use it and traffic congestion grew accordingly. This had a disastrous impact on the bus services, whose average commercial speed in the peak period within Paris dropped from 14km/hr in 1952 to 10km/hr in 1965, the latter figure being almost exactly that of the horse buses of the CGO in the 1890s. The number of passengers using the bus network declined in almost exact proportion. From 1961 to 1971 it fell progressively from 796 million to 514 million and had gone down to exactly 500 million two years later. During the same period, the total of vehicle kilometres actually increased slightly, from 117.5 million to 119.2 million. Costs and thus losses increased in inverse proportion. Until the mid-1960s, losses on the road services could be covered from the surplus earned by the rail network, but it too then began to lose traffic and cross-subsidisation could no longer be applied. Clearly something had to be done if Paris and its surrounding region were to retain any kind of bus service at all and, in conjunction with the sometimes-reluctant municipal authorities, the RATP began to study measures which would reduce costs and also give the bus a degree of priority and help to reverse the decline.

Although a plan drawn up by the municipality in 1959 had first mentioned the importance of giving the bus priority, nothing actually happened until 15th January 1964 when a bus lane, 990m long and 3m wide, was instituted along the quays between Châtelet and Place du Carrousel. Its success was immediate and on the six lines which passed along it, speeds rose by 75% and there was a great reduction in delays. There was also, however, a good deal of opposition from shopkeepers, businesses along the line of proposed corridors and taxi drivers, although that of the last of these evaporated within a short time as bus lanes were opened to them also. While this silenced their protests, it also slightly reduced the average speed of the buses using the lanes.

ABOVE: TN 4 H, 3458, is well and truly stuck in a traffic jam on the Boulevard Haussmann c1968. Behind, Somua OPS 3 809 is not making any better progress. *(J-B Prudhommeaux, collection Assa)*

BELOW: The traditional method of boarding became less safe as traffic increased. A crowd of home-going commuters, having arrived by Métro line 8, prepare to board TN 4 A2 ,1706, at Porte Dorée on 20th July 1955. The building in the background was then known as the Musée de France d'Outre-mer, and on that date housed an exhibition on the works of Jules Verne. *(Author)*

There was also a problem of illegal parking and by 1970 it was found that parking restrictions would have to be much more strictly enforced if the bus lanes were to work properly. Given these problems, the authorities were not immediately convinced of their usefulness and it was not until after 1975 that any significant number of lanes was in operation. On lanes opened at a later date, the width was increased form 3m to 3.5m, to allow the buses to travel faster without endangering vehicles on the rest of the road.

BELOW: In April 1968 Standard 2619 travels along the-then new contra-flow bus lane on the Boulevard Saint-Germain. The sign on the pole warns pedestrians of *"Autobus à contresens"* (buses running against the traffic). *(Author)*

The other major development of this period was the introduction of buses of the Standard design, covered more fully in the section on rolling stock. The large-scale introduction of new buses was made possible only by the greatly increased level of finance made available to the RATP by the government and by what was then known as the District, later the Région of Ile-de-France. While most of this went on the RER, a small part also found its way to the road network.

In June 1969 the first trials of a radio-telephone system between drivers and a central control point took place on three city and four suburban lines. As these proved to be successful in increasing punctuality, the system was in 1972 extended to most of the urban lines and to some in the suburbs, before being further extended to the entire network between 1977 and 1979. From 1990 onwards, liaison between regulators and bus drivers has been further improved by the introduction of a global positioning satellite system (GPS), linked also to an information system known as Système d'Information en Ligne (SIEL) (Line Information System). This allows regulators to adjust the service to cope with any problems, by such methods as turning vehicles short when service has been interrupted. This system also functions as a real time information system, to keep passengers updated on the current running of services. Regulators operate from one of 70 Postes de Commandement Locale (PCL) (Local Control Centres), most of these being located at important terminal points, although some are now based in depots. There is a separate security system, Aide à l'Intervention Globale sur les Lignes en Exploitation (AIGLE) (System to provide assistance on lines which are in service), which can be activated by the setting off of an alarm by the driver and which then leads to liaison with the police. All buses and trams are equipped with cctv video systems.

As will be seen in the fleet history, the fleet had contained buses operated by (at that time always) one man since the 1920s, but these had always been confined to services in relatively quiet suburbs and had not always been popular with passengers. In 1967, Dr Simon Nora, chair of a commission set up in the previous year to examine productivity in industries controlled by the public sector, had been highly critical of the generally low level of productivity and, while not completely in agreement with his comments, Pierre Weil showed that he was willing to take significant steps to improve matters. For the road services this meant the conversion of the entire network to driver-only operation (since 1963 women had been employed as drivers), and to allow this, the tariff system had first to be simplified, as detailed elsewhere. There was naturally a good deal of anxiety among the personnel, in particular among conductors, of whom there were 4,500 in 1967. Negotiations with the trade unions resulted in a protocol, signed on 9th July 1970, which allayed the concerns of the conductors and also served as a basis for discussions with staff in other branches of the RATP. Some conductors had already left voluntarily and 1,400 went in the year following the agreement. By 31st July 1972 all urban services, with the exception of the PC, had been converted and the latter was finally converted in February 1973. The system was then extended to the suburbs and the changeover was completed by 1st June 1974. Most of the conductors went on to become drivers. The conversion was accompanied by a gratifying reduction in costs on the road services.

While bus lanes had certainly helped to accelerate the services and reduce delays, it was recognised that their usefulness was limited by their short length and it was decided to put a more ambitious concept into operation on some lines, designated "Lignes Pilotes". On these lanes extended for at least 50% of the length of the line. The first went into operation in the last months of 1973, when eight lines were re-routed to use bus lanes for much of their length. The results were excellent, with average speeds rising and passenger numbers increasing by around 20%. From 1976 these lines were normally worked by standard buses which had been upgraded to provide an improved level of comfort.

Much the same aim was behind the introduction of priority at traffic lights, first introduced in 1974. The first installations were at Neuilly (lines 163 and 164), at Boulevard Barbès (lines 31 and 56) and at the intersection of the Avenue Simon Bolivar and the Rue de Belleville (line 26). However, there was no change in the basic pattern of services and no equivalent of London's Bus Reshaping Plan.

These measures, together with the introduction of the *Carte Orange* on 1st July 1975 (fully described in the section on tickets and fares), were clearly successful in arresting the decline of bus patronage within the city, where the number of passengers carried increased from 223 million in 1975 to 324 million in 1980, it was another story in the suburbs. While the number of lines there had increased from 80 in 1950 to 175 in 1987, the total number of passengers carried had scarcely increased at all, rising only from 345 million in 1975 to 409 million in 1980. For both inter-suburban commuting and for leisure traffic the, car with almost 87.2% of all traffic in 1983/4, had won hands down. The RATP decided to challenge this and in 1987 divided the suburban area into 15 zones, to allow a greater degree of local management. This was followed two years later by the launch of

At the same time, under the various governments of President Mitterand, official attitudes had changed considerably. In the Economic Plan for 1989-1993, transport had priority and public transport received an allocation of seven milliard* francs annually. While this was still less than the amount given to roads (11 milliard), the gap between the two had closed considerably since the 1960s. For the road services, most of this money was used to finance the construction of the Trans Val-de-Marne bus corridor, generally known as TVM. Opened in 1993, this runs in the eastern suburbs, to run between Saint-Maur and Rungis and is now worked by articulated vehicles. It has proved successful in bringing to bus passengers many of the benefits of a light rail service. An extension of 15km eastwards from Saint-Maur to Noisy-le-Grand has been proposed for some years, but met initially with opposition for the mayor of Saint-Maur. It does not feature in present official plans, but may be revived in 2011.

One of the busiest services and also one which was most prone to delays caused by congestion was the circular PC (Petite Ceinture) service, which had replaced the trains of the railway line of the same name in 1934. It was worked as a complete circle, although buses and crews had a break at Porte d'Ivry, while passengers made a mad dash for the bus waiting in front. It had almost immediately more than trebled the number of passengers carried, to 16 million. However, as traffic grew and road congestion increased, the drawbacks of working this line as a single service became obvious and in October 1999 it was split into three separate, over-lapping services, designated PC1, 2 and 3. More bus lanes were created and the stopping places were equipped with real-time information equipment. While this certainly improved the regularity of the service, it was still clear that on some sections, a form of rapid transit was required to cope with the demand and in December 2006 most of line PC1, which served the southern portion of the circle, was replaced by tram line T3, which will be extended in the near future to replace all of line PC2 and part of PC3 (*q.v.* tramway extensions).

In the last few years, two campaigns have been instituted to improve the image of the bus and the quality of service offered. The first, *"Bus Attitude"* was set up in 2003, initially on ten lines serving the north-west of the city, such as line 65 (Aubervilliers – Gare de Lyon). It was aimed to improve passenger behaviour and, in particular, check on fraudulent travel. In this latter it has been fairly successful, the incidence of such travel having declined from an estimated 16% of total passenger numbers to 10.2%. The other campaign has been a joint operation between RATP, STIF and the regional authority of Ile-de-France. Known as Mobilien, it is intended to improve the speed, regularity and attractiveness of bus services, as part of a larger aim to reduce car travel by 3% in the Region. More bus lanes are created along the routes of the services so designated, stops are re-located to bring them closer to passengers' destinations and further priority is given at traffic lights. In connection with this campaign, interchange points will be made more attractive to passengers and real time information on the running of services will be made available to passengers. Before a line is so treated, there are detailed discussions with local authorities, local business, educational establishments and other interested parties. As this process takes time, only a few lines, including line 38 and the PC services, have so far been converted, but it is hoped to have 30 lines in service in the near future and, ultimately, 70.

"Autrement Bus" (A different kind of bus), an exercise intended to make Franciliens view the bus in a more positive light and so to increase their use of it. The project, first tried in Hautes-de-Seine, aimed to present information in a much more accessible form and also to involve individual depots in the promotion of their services. More inter-suburban lines were put into service, such as line 394 which now runs from Bourg-le-Reine in the south to Issy-les-Moulineaux in the south-west, a distance of 12km. In co-operation with local authorities, a large number of bus-priority schemes were created. Service letters were replaced by numbers and each line was given a colour code. All this required a budget of between 40 and 50 million francs per annum during the development of the project. Implementation began in 1989 in Bagneux, Châtillon and Clamart and was gradually extended across the entire network in the next nine ten years. It had moderate success in attracting passengers out of their cars and on to the buses and by 1993 the suburban network was carrying 508 million passengers; the new suburban tram lines, however, had much greater success.

Services have also been developed to take the bus into parts of the city, generally areas with narrow streets and tight bends, which have not previously been served. A service in Montmartre, known as 'Montmartrobus' had been inaugurated as far back as 10th February 1983, using, initially, Renault minibuses (11–38). It was a success, especially with tourists, and in due course the minibuses were replaced by midi-

*Milliard is a French-derived word and is the correct rendering of the number 1,000,000,000 (one thousand million). It is not normally used in English.

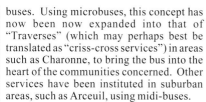

buses. Using microbuses, this concept has now been now expanded into that of "Traverses" (which may perhaps best be translated as "criss-cross services") in areas such as Charonne, to bring the bus into the heart of the communities concerned. Other services have been instituted in suburban areas, such as Arceuil, using midi-buses.

While it is as yet too early to assess the results of Mobilien, it is clear that, as it approaches its 180th birthday, the Paris bus is now increasingly valued by both public authorities as a means of controlling the growth of road traffic and of improving the urban environment, while passengers now see it as a comfortable and useful means of travel. It is no longer the poor relation of the city's transport. Although the developing tramways and the Métro will have the major share of infrastructure funds in the next few years, the bus network will also benefit by the extensions of busways listed below. These come under the general heading of TCSP, *Transports en commun en site propre* (public transport on reserved right of way).:-

1. Already under construction is a line from Massy-Palaiseau (RER line B) to Saclay. Of its length of 6.3km, 3.3km will be on busway.

2. Also under construction is a line from Sucy-Bonneuil (RER line A) to Créteil (parc des Sports, future extension of Métro line 8) and Pompadour (future station on RER line D). It should be ready at the beginning of 2011.

3. A line in the outer south-west suburbs from Sénart to Evry via Corbeil. This line of 13km has also been considered for tram-train operation, but it now seems likely that it will initially be worked by buses on their own right of way, as far as Corbeil, to be opened in 2010. This may later become a trolleybus route and the link onwards to Evry a tramway, to be built by the Syndicat Mixte de transports Essonne, a departmental body.

4. A local line in the Versailles area, of 7.5km length, to link that town with Le Chesnay and serve the three RER stations in Versailles (Rive Droite, Rive Gauche and Chantiers).

5. A line to be constructed under the Plan Espoir Banlieue scheme (*q.v.* tramways), to run between RER line D at Villiers-le-Bel and RER line B at Parc des Expositions via Gonesse. This is planned for 2015 but may be ready earlier and at a later date it may be converted to some form of rail transport.

ABOVE: Heuliez midi-bus 457 on line V1, at Hôtel de Ville d'Arceuil, in the southern suburbs, on 16th April 2008. It is wearing a special livery for the Val de Bièvre service, which runs on a circular route around Arceuil and is one of several local services which have been introduced with support from the local authority of the area. *(Author)*

RIGHT: Gruau microbus 737 at la Chapelle on the Traverse Ney-Flandre on 16th April 2008. At this point line 2 of the Métro runs on viaduct and the station can be seen behind. *(Author)*

BELOW: Mercedes-Benz minibus 840 awaits departure from the bus station at Châtillon-Montrouge, terminus of Métro line 13 on 20th September 2008. It is working on circular line 323. *(Author)*

Fleet History

Horse Buses

The original horse buses were all single-deckers. The very first to be placed in service by Baudry in 1828 followed closely the design of the contemporary diligence (stage coach), with three separate internal compartments. This arrangement proved to be unsuitable for urban work and was soon replaced by a single inner saloon. Entry was by a door in the rear of the vehicle and the conductor led a precarious existence clinging to the rear step. There were usually three side windows and the interior was somewhat claustrophobic. Seating capacity was usually 14 or 16. Three horses were used to pull the vehicle. By 1840 some companies were running buses with five side windows and a brighter and more airy interior.

The first real innovation came in 1853, when double-deckers appeared on the streets. These had a knifeboard seat on the upper deck, access to which was gained by an iron ladder and this deck was reserved for male passengers, although it is unlikely that ladies in fashionable crinolines could have managed the ladder in any case. The fact that fares on the upper deck were lower than those charged 'inside' went some way to make up for the complete lack of protection from the weather. The upper deck allowed the carriage of an additional 12 passengers and thus improved the economics of horse bus operation.

The newly-formed CGO inherited a varied, and generally obsolete fleet from the various smaller companies and, as one of the conditions of its concession was that it should modernise the fleet, it at once set about producing a modern, standard vehicle, the first of which appeared in 1856. These were designed following requirements laid down by the Prefect of the Seine. The new buses were constructed in the Company's own workshops and it adopted the double-deck concept with enthusiasm, no single-deckers being used within Paris for many years thereafter. In this design, the saloon had six side windows and a fair amount of headroom and total capacity was 24. This design was multiplied in great numbers and remained in production until 1878. In 1867 a new bus cost FR3,500 – this would have been about £350 – using high quality materials and built by highly skilled (and paid) craftsmen.

By the early 1860s there were 569 in service. In 1878 a new and larger design appeared, when the CGO took horse-bus technology to its limits by placing in service the first of its 40-seater vehicles. These required three horses and were used only on the most heavily-trafficked lines, such as line E, Madeleine-Bastille, or on lines serving the International Exposition of that year. From this date buses had a proper stair leading to the upper deck which latter women were now allowed to use. Photographic evidence suggests that they took to it with enthusiasm.

24. Paris Vécu. — Les Voyageurs pour l'impériale

L. J. & Cⁱᵉ, édit. Angoulême-Paris

It may be questioned whether the extra capacity of the larger buses produced any additional revenue, as the placing of one of them into service required the purchase and feeding of ten additional horses. One such bus, if filled to capacity for most of the time on most journeys, might have produced an additional FR35 per day or FR12,775 per year. Against this there would have been the cost of extra fodder (FR26 per day or FR9,490 per year), plus the first cost of the horses (FR300, assuming a working life of ten years). There would also have been the cost of the construction of additional stabling to house them. It was, at best, a finely-balanced equation, but no doubt the increased capacity of the new buses helped the CGO to cope with peak periods, such as occurred on Sundays, and so to fulfil the obligations laid down in its concession. Neither in London

ABOVE: Several lady passengers seem determined to take advantage of their recently-won freedom to travel on the top deck, in this view of a two-horse bus on line F, Place Wagram – Bastille. Clad in a kind of Inverness cape, the conductor looks on and perhaps wonders just how long the bus will have to wait! (*Author's collection*)

RIGHT: One of the three-horse vehicles, wearing the brown livery, awaits departure from the station in Pl de Batignolles, on a day which was sunny enough for top deck passengers to need the shade of a parasol. (*Author's collection*)

32. PARIS XVIⁱ. — Place et square des Batignolles
Station des Omnibus

Cadot, Paris

ABOVE: Preserved two-horse vehicle no.2177, beautifully restored by AMUTIR, in Colombes museum in September 2002. *(Author)*

RIGHT: The buses operated by the railway companies have already been mentioned. On this post card, dated 1902, one, operated by the Chemins de Fer de l'Ouest, is seen at the intersection of the Bd Saint-Denis and the Bd de Strasbourg. It is painted green, fitted with a light awning roof and the arrangement of the platform is rather different to that on the CGO buses. *(Author's collection)*

nor Berlin was any attempt made to copy the example of Paris. In 1888 there was a reversion to smaller, two-horse vehicles, seating 30 and this type remained the standard until the motor bus arrived after 1906. To the end, horse buses in Paris had knifeboard seating on the upper deck; the garden seat layout, which was used in London from the 1880s, was not at any time seen on Paris horse buses.

Mechanical propulsion

The first mechanically-propelled bus to operate in the area was actually a kind of road train, the Train-Scotte, which ran briefly between Pont de Neuilly and Colombes from 7th or 8th April to a date in May 1897. This consisted of a steam tractor with 12 places for passengers, towing a two-axle trailer which could seat 24. Both vehicles were single-deckers. There were also brief trials with a Weidknecht steam bus which had a double-deck body from a CGO horse bus. An electric trolleybus was tried between Porte de Vincennes and Lac Daumesnil during the exposition of 1900. More successful was a Gardner-Serpollet steam bus which worked on line AM (Montmartre – Saint-Germain-des Près in July 1905.

The CGO was watching the development of the motor vehicle with close interest and in 1904 invited manufacturers to produce prototypes of *"omnibus automobiles"* which would be suitable for service in Paris. Nine builders accepted the challenge and in the autumn of 1905 delivered their sample products. All were double-deckers and all looked alike, the bodies being built by the CGO in its own workshops, based

closely on those fitted to horse buses, but fitted with a roof over the upper deck. The manufacturers concerned were Brillié, Delehaye, De Dion, Krieger, Mag, Mors, NAG (German, the only foreign entrant), Peugeot, Serpollet and Turgan. The vehicle by De Dion was a petrol-electric and that by Serpollet was the steam bus mentioned above; all the others were conventional motor vehicles. Some other double-deckers, with different bodywork, were tried on other lines and a Turgan of somewhat British appearance ran on line C from Porte de Neuilly to Palais Royal. With all the prototypes, a service was provided during the Paris motor show of 1905, from 8th to 24th December. This event was held in the Grand Palais and the buses ran to and from the Bourse. The venture was clearly a success and based on the experience gained, the CGO ordered 150 of Brillié type P2 (2-151) to begin regular service in 1906. These had Schneider engines and the bodies were again similar to those of the horse buses. The prototype of this type was taken into the fleet as no.1

Unlike the ABOAG in Berlin, the CGO was in no way tentative about the beginning of regular commercial service, which took place on Monday 11th June 1906, at 06.00. The eleven buses to be used on line AM assembled at Montmartre terminus and the first bus left at 06.14, to make its way to Saint-Germain-des-Prés in exactly 27 minutes, about half the time taken by horse buses on the same journey. The CGO referred to the buses as 'omnibus automobiles' and that wording was carried on the new stop signs, attached to the gas lamps, but Parisians very soon shortened this to 'autobus', thus giving a new word not only to French but also to most other European languages. The fleet was garaged at Clichy depot. Between June 1906 and 30th June 1907 the P2s were successively introduced on six other lines. On the whole the new buses performed well, but as early as July 1906 the CGO received a sharp letter from the City asking them to provide windscreens on the upper deck and to do something to lessen vibration, particularly on the platforms. The first point was addressed by the fitting of a bulkhead, with two large windows, to the front of the upper deck, with seating capacity increased to 16. The rubber blocks fitted to the wheels were replaced by solid rubber tyres, in an attempt to cure the vibration, but these still left much to be desired. However, in view of the approaching end of the Company's concession, there was no move to expand the fleet and it is clear that the services were still regarded as experimental. There were problems with the suspension, which was distinctly hard, but the operator was unwilling to improve this, as there were also problems of stability, due to the overall height of the buses. By 1908 the CGO had decided that the double-decker was not the most suitable type for urban operation and the last ran in December 1911.

ABOVE: The Krieger prototype on the demonstration service to the motor show in December 1905. *(Author's collection)*
BELOW: By 1908 a certain amount of motor traffic had appeared on the Bd des Italiens, including double-decker 115. The original rear wheels with rubber blocks can clearly be seen and some motor cars can be distinguished to the rear, but there are still plenty of horse buses around. *(Author's collection)*

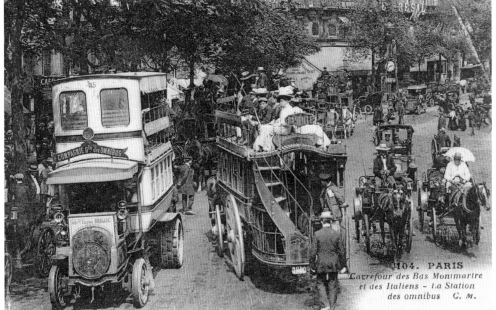

Various manufacturers were then invited to submit models of single-deck designs and between that year and 1910 five builders delivered nine prototypes, which then underwent extensive trials in service. The manufacturers concerned were Brillié, Brasier, Renault and de Dion Bouton. A variety of different body designs was offered – the Brasier had a central entrance, but most had an open rear

platform with side access or the same with rear access. The Brillié vehicle, which was mounted on a P2 chassis, simply had a door in the rear bulkhead and no platform at all. The Renault was tried with pneumatic tyres, but these were judged to be unsuccessful. In 1909 Schneider delivered two buses with rear platforms, one having a side entrance and one having the entrance in the middle of the rear, with boarding from the roadway. There was also a De Dion with central entrance. After all had undergone extensive trials, mostly on line H between Avenue de Clichy and Odéon, it was decided to standardise on the open rear platform with end access, on Schneider and De Dion vehicles, and so was launched the design which was to symbolise Paris for the next forty years and which would not finally disappear from service until 1971.

The first series of buses to this layout was the class of Schneider PB2, the first of which entered service in 1911. This firm had in the meantime taken over Brillié. Total capacity was 35, divided between two classes, with two different arrangements of seating, either 16/19 or 12/23. There were five side windows, arranged differently depending on the internal layout. This class ultimately numbered 627 vehicles (201-718 and 801-910), To the same basic design was the de Dion Bouton DA class, of which there were 263 examples (1001-1263) and which could be distinguished from the PB2 design by having one large and four smaller side windows. This type was also very slightly shorter, at 6.91m, and could seat 31 passengers. Also in 1911 came either 97 or 100 of class Brillié-Schneider P3 (1-97 or 1-100, sources differ). These re-used the chassis of withdrawn double-deckers, slightly lengthened to 6.66m and, in some cases also, the lower saloons. Others had new bodies. This was a slightly smaller bus, with a capacity of 30 passengers. All these classes ran on solid rubber tyres and the driving position was totally exposed to the elements. With these buses, the CGO was able to replace all its horse-drawn vehicles and by 1914 had a total of 1,045 vehicles, serving 42 lines.

All of these buses disappeared abruptly from the city's streets in August 1914, when they were requisitioned by the army. Many were converted into supply vehicles and fitted to carry 1,800kg of meat. The side windows were removed and replaced by metal panels. Others were used as troop transports in the area of the front line or as ambulances. The Paris bus certainly played a distinguished part in the Battle of the Marne and helped to save the city and the country from invasion. In Paris, passengers had to make do with the trams and the Métro and some journeys, such as that from Saint-Lazare to Gare du Nord, became quite difficult, especially for military personnel laden with kit bags. The CGO pressed the government to be allowed to resume some services with new buses and, after some wrangling, it gained its point.

Work then went ahead on the next design of bus and the first of the Schneider H type appeared on the streets on 1st June 1916, on the Madeleine-Bastille line E, and ultimately the delivery of this type allowed resumption of service on four lines. Deliveries continued at an increased pace after the war and a total of 1269 (1-1269) was ultimately acquired. No other city had put so many buses of a single type into service at that time. Buses of this design could carry 38 passengers in total – seating was for 16 and 12, in first and second class respectively, and ten standees could be carried on the rear platform.

ABOVE: A Schneider PB2 at Saint-Lazare about 1912, with the Hôtel Terminus behind and a fair amount of other motor traffic in the street. *(Author's collection)*

RIGHT: The worst accident in the history of the bus in Paris happened on 27th September 1911 when a bus of this type fell into the Seine at Pont de l'Archivéché. Eleven passengers were drowned and the incident, as well as the subsequent salvage of the wreck, aroused much interest. A disaster was always good for the sale of post cards and this publisher clearly moved quickly, since the card was written just three days later. *(Author's collection)*

PARIS - 27 Septembre 1911 — L'ACCIDENT DU PONT DE L'ARCHEVÉCHÉ
UN AUTOBUS DANS LA SEINE - 11 Morts — L'Autobus soulevé émerge des flots

BELOW: How to board one of the first single-deckers, c1912. A three-horse bus passes on the right. *(Author's collection)*

20

RIGHT: De Dion-Bouton DA, 1215, negotiates Place de la Concorde about 1912. *(Author's collection)*

3690 — PARIS.
Fontaines jaillissantes de la Place de la Concorde.   ND Phot.

BELOW: H class 534 as preserved, on the return working of the centenary parade on 15 October 2006. It is climbing the ramp to Pont de l'Alma, with the underpass to the right *(Author)*

BOTTOM: In a posed photograph of the mid-1920s, a splendidly-bewhiskered gendarme holds up the traffic at Porte Saint-Denis, including H6 5009, working on line E to Bastille. Unfortunately the build-up of the traffic has hidden the rear wheels. *(Author's collection)*

BOTTOM RIGHT: An interesting view from above of two H class buses, at an unknown location in the 1920s. *(Author's collection)*

A sloping metal cover gave the driver rather more protection than he had hitherto enjoyed. From 1929 many were given pneumatic tyres and the class remained in service until 1938. This class had a slightly rounded roof, rather than the clerestory of earlier designs, and prominent roller blind indicators. With it came the helpful practice, still continued to the present day, of displaying termini and intermediate points on a band along the side of the bus below the saloon windows. One bus of this type has been preserved.

An enlarged variant appeared in 1923, the H6, a six-wheeler which could take 56 passengers altogether, 48 of these seated (20 and 28). Unlike contemporary six-wheel designs in Britain, this design did not use a rear bogie but had a central axle, which could turn independently of the others. Despite this feature, the buses lacked manoeuvrability and were confined to two lines, E and AK (Gare St Lazare-Gare du Nord) which ran on wide boulevards in the city centre. They had an ungainly appearance and, as only 51 (5001-5051) were built, it can be assumed that they were not altogether successful.

In 1924 the firm of Schneider was taken over by Somua but the management of the STCRP seemed not to favour the new owners and instead looked to Renault for most of its future deliveries. Only 15 small buses, of type MAT2 (6001-6015), were supplied by Somua at this time, along with 15 Renault class KX1 (6016-6030). Both types were known as the "Express", since they operated express journeys, at higher fares, on some of the busier lines. Seating accommodation was one-class only and provided for 25, no standing passengers being carried. They were designed for driver-only operation and the driver benefited from the protection of a full windscreen. These were the first buses to be fitted with pneumatic tyres. The express services were not a success and were withdrawn at the end of 1925.

However, in 1927 Renault arrived in Paris on a much larger scale when the first PN took to the streets and ultimately no fewer than 337 (1301-1667) were in service, the last not being withdrawn until 1950. By comparison with earlier designs, the PN was much lower and there

0834. NEUILLY-sur-SEINE
Avenue du Roule à l'Avenue Sainte-Foy   E. M.

ABOVE: A PN seen at Neuilly about 1929 while working on pre-war line C. *(AMTUIR, collection Assa)*

was no longer an intermediate step from street level to the rear platform. It was also wider, at 2.37m. These improvements allowed the carriage of 39 passengers in total, 28 being seated (16 and 12) and eleven standees could be taken on the platform. This type did not have a radiator in the conventional position, since this was placed behind a grille on the side of the bus. Originally mounted on solid tyres, these buses were soon given pneumatic tyres but, although they lasted in service until 1950, they were not fitted with windscreens after the war. One, 1347, has been preserved by AMTUIR.

In 1929 there arrived a smaller Renault product, with 23 buses of type PY (6031-6053). These were mainly used in the suburbs, although they also worked on a line to the Sacré Coeur on Montmartre during the closure of the funicular *(q.v.)*. They were operated by one man and 38 passengers could be carried. One was briefly converted to run as a trolleybus, but without success. These buses lasted until 1939. Both Renault and Somua also supplied to the STCRP a series of touring coaches with folding roofs, based on the Express design, for use on city sightseeing tours.

The success of classes PN and PY marked the beginning of a long association between the STCRP and (later) the RATP and Renault and in 1931 the next main series began to enter service. This was the TN 4 A2, of which there were 320 examples (1638-1957), most of these being used on tramway replacement. Again this was a larger vehicle than its predecessor and capacity was now 50, with 33 seated (17 and 16). It also featured twin headlamps, in anticipation of the compulsory introduction of these later in the '30s. Unfortunately the engine on this type proved to be rather prone to failure and all had to be re-engined in 1938. Those which survived the war were given drivers' windscreens and the last was withdrawn in 1959. A version was also built for suburban service, classified TN 4 A1, intended for one-man operation. There were 150 of these (6054-6203). Passengers entered by a folding door at the front and the driver had a completely enclosed cabin from the beginning. The rear platform was totally enclosed. The engines showed the same weakness as on the TN 4 A 2 class and were likewise replaced in 1938. In 1950 the whole class was converted to the design of TN 4 B and in this form lasted

until 1959. Outwardly identical to class TN 4 A2 was type TN 6 A2, which first appeared in 1932 and which ultimately numbered 770 vehicles (1958-2727). These had six-cylinder engines and their extra power proved to be most useful on hilly routes in the north of the city. The suburban version had a different interior layout and could carry more passengers, (57 against 50) but all were worked with a conductor. A slightly modernised design appeared in 1934, the TN 6 C2, of which there were 160 (2728-2887), intended for suburban operation. These were fitted with a windscreen from new, although the sides of the driving position remained open. These buses were later given diesel engines, by either Panhard or Hispano Hercules and the driving positions were completely enclosed on those vehicles which survived the war. The last survivors were withdrawn in 1969. There was also a one-man operated suburban version, the TN 6 C 1 Banlieue, of which there were 90 (6204-6293). These buses had an enclosed body and driving cab and a single-width door at the front and were known by the travelling public as "cages à poules" (hen coops). Mechanically the two versions were identical and the TN 6 C1 version lasted in traffic until 1959.

There was then a reversion to four-cylinder engines with classes TN 4 C and TN 4 F of 1934-5. Both used the bodywork of the TN 6 C2, although with some detail differences, and both gave excellent service, not being withdrawn until 1959 and 1970 respectively. Total numbers were 50 (2938-2987) and 285 (2988-3272). At the same time, what appeared to be the monopoly of Renault was interrupted by the purchase of two batches from Panhard. There were 50 of class K 63 A (2888-2937) and 65 of K 63 B (3273-3337). The bodywork was identical to that fitted to the various contemporary

BELOW: A TN 4 A 2 passes the Printemps department store on the Boulevard Haussmann about 1935. It is working on tramway replacement line BO, formerly tram line 15. Due to increasing traffic, the *"passage clouté"* (pedestrian crossing marked by studs in the roadway) has come into use and pedestrians are clearly taking advantage of it. *(AMTUIR, collection Assa)*

BOTTOM: Preserved TN 6 C1 6284 in the Saint-Mandé museum. *(Author)*

boulevard Haussmann - vers 1931
Collection T. ASSA
AMTUIR ©

22

Renault classes. However, they did not last as long and the last ran in 1952. Both manufacturers also supplied in 1935 twelve each of a design of small one-man operated buses, and the Renault design looked very like London Transport's Leyland Cubs. Those by Renault were classified ZYAE (6294-6303), while those by Panhard were ZUROC (6304-6313). The results of this experiment seem to have been unsatisfactory and these buses did not run after 1939.

Leaving aside these last two classes, the STCRP had placed in service between 1932 and 1935 exactly 1700 buses of virtually identical design. Most of these were used on tramway replacement services and they also replaced the Petite Ceinture railway line in 1934. To the average passenger, whether Parisian or tourist, these became the typical Paris bus and, perhaps because of their longevity, they have continued to enjoy that honour to the present day. They were robust vehicles, having the advantage that, both mechanically and physically, they were relatively easy to maintain by depot staff and visits to the central workshops were infrequent. This certainly proved a boon during the war years, but their very strength later told against them. By 1960 they looked antiquated when seen alongside the sleek new cars with which they shared the streets and the traditional rear entrance became more and more of a bottleneck, with passengers queuing in the roadway to board their bus.

The STCRP, however, did not intend to rest on its laurels and in March 1936 placed in service the first of a new design of bus, the Renault TN 4 H. This was slightly longer than the previous standard design and had a five-bay body, the tops of the windows being rounded. The most striking feature, however, was the absence of the projecting bonnet, since the driver now sat over the engine, rather than behind it. The rear platform was still open, but shorter and seating capacity could be correspondingly increased. There were 410 of this class, TN4 H P, (3338-3597 and 3978-4127). Very shortly afterwards a suburban version appeared with an enclosed platform. Some of these retained the traditional entrance position and were classified TN 4 H BAR (Banlieu, Accèss Arrière), (3829-3831, 4258-4277 and 4298-4247). Most, however, had the entrance in the side of the platform and were classified TN 4 H BAL (Banlieu, Accès Latéral), (3658-3828, 3832-3917, 4128-4257, 4278-4297). To the passenger, the most welcome development was the fitting of rubber cushions on the seats of this class. In view of the size of the order, 970 vehicles in all, not all bodies were constructed by the STCRP, some being by MGT (Millon-Guiet-Tubauto) and others by CIV (Carrosserie Industrielle de Versailles). From photographs. it would seem that there was a certain amount of exchange of bodies and chassis over the years. The last TN 4 H was withdrawn in 1971.

Panhard again managed to secure a contract from the STCRP and in 1937 there appeared the first of a total of 220 buses, of classes K 63 C and K 63 B. These corresponded in design exactly to the Renault designs and the total was sub-divided into 60 for use in Paris (3598-

TOP LEFT: TN 4 F 3012 awaits its next turn of duty at Pigalle in April 1968. *(Author)*

ABOVE LEFT: A scene in the rue de Rivoli on 18th April 1968. Buses take advantage of a new bus lane and nearest the camera TN 4 F 3099 shows off the traditional rear entrance, while beyond is TN 4 H 4094. *(Author)*

LEFT: TN 4 H 4097 crosses the Pont de la Concorde in April 1968, followed by a post-was Chausson. *(Author)*

BELOW LEFT: A scene at a stop in April 1968 with a member of class TN 4 HB designed for suburban operation, but by this time running in the city. The narrow doorway was a distinct drawback in city traffic. *(Author)*

BELOW: A TN 4 H is seen at the Louvre in April 1968, contrasting with the futuristic lines of the Saviem double-deck sightseeing coach belonging to Cityrama on the right. *(Author)*

3657) and 160 (3918-3977 and 4428-4527) for suburban operation. The former were the last buses to be built with the typical open rear platform. These vehicles were quieter in operation than the corresponding Renaults, but their engines were rather delicate and could not be converted for gas operation during the war, when all were stored out of service. They also had shorter lives than their Renault counterparts and the last was taken out of service in 1955.

At the outbreak of war in 1939, the STCRP had at its disposal a fleet of almost 3,500 buses, of which 85% had been built in the last seven years. Most of these were requisitioned in 1939 and saw service as troop carriers, food supply vehicles and ambulances. Many were returned after the armistice of June 1940, but having some buses at its disposal was not the end of the problem for the STCRP, as fuel was virtually unobtainable and on 10th July 1940 it was decided to experiment with the use of town gas as a replacement fuel. The workshop staff went to work with record speed and in August two buses, fitted with enormous containers on their roofs, appeared on line 39. They seemed to work well and by the end of the year, 500 had been similarly treated and a charging point installed at the city terminus of Porte de Clichy. With these it was possible to maintain a service on eight lines within Paris and 36 in the suburbs. These filled the very few gaps in the Metro system, which otherwise had to cope with the entire urban traffic during the Occupation. The Germans were sufficiently impressed to pay the designers the compliment of taking copies of the plans with which to modify buses in German cities. About 300 others were fitted with gas generators which burned wood (120), coke or minerals (180) and redundant personnel were sent off to the provinces on numerous tree-cutting expeditions. These latter fuels were much less reliable and often failed in service. Yet others, 274 in all, were converted to run on ethyl-alcohol and by 1944 these maintained almost all services, the gas buses having given up the unequal struggle. Apart from the question of fuel, it was by this time very difficult to obtain new tyres.

Early Post-War Buses

When Paris was liberated in August 1944, only 1145 buses remained and only 435 of these were in serviceable condition. A mammoth search operation was mounted, not only within France but also in Belgium and North Africa, and, later, in the French zones of Germany and Austria. After two years, almost 1,000 mostly decrepit buses had been located and returned to Paris but it was recognised that that would be the maximum which could be rehabilitated and that new vehicles would have to be bought soon in considerable quantity. To this end, the technical staff began work on a prototype, numbered 6001, which appeared on the road on 15th August 1947. Mechanically it was based on the Renault TN4 H, with a lengthened chassis, but it had a body of a completely new and most attractive design, with power-operated doors and passenger flow from rear to front. There were 38 seats. Two other prototypes (6002/3) were built by outside builders, 6002 being a prototype Somua OP5, with chassis number 90000 and MGT (Million-Guiet-Tubauto) bodywork. It later became 53 in the training fleet and survived until 1969. 6003 was built by SNCASO (Société Nouvelle de Constructions Aéronautiques du Sud-Ouest) and had a Panhard diesel engine. All these buses also had a doorway on the offside, behind the back axle, as did the later OP5/2.

However, the pressing need in 1947 was to put new buses on the road as quickly as possible, without waiting for the results of extended road tests and on 24th June 1947 the first of a series of new vehicles took to the road. This was a Chausson APH 47, which was essentially a coach — it did not even possess a box for the line number — and 18 of these (1-18) went into service on suburban line 285 (Porte d'Italie – Savigny-sur-Orge). These were for driver-only operation and only the single-width front door was used in service, apart from unloading at terminal points. They were followed in 1948 by 32 (19-50) identical vehicles, also used on suburban services. These were the first buses to be commissioned by the new RATP. Next came four (51-54) with a folding rear door in place of the outward-opening one of the first batches. Finally in 1952 there arrived 18 of type APH 2.50 (55-72).

Central Paris had to wait until 1950 to see its first post-war series of buses. In that year the first of 301 Somua OP5-2 buses (501-801) entered service. This design was based closely on the prototype, 6002, of 1947 and was really the first modern bus to run in central Paris, but, although providing much improved comfort, it somehow lacked the appeal of the pre-war models. While it was easier for conductors to collect fares from a fixed post, rather than by struggling up and down a crowded gangway, some found that the contact was now much too brief and formal and lamented that they coudl no longer get to know regulars. These buses had a rear entrance and front exit, with a fixed post provided for the conductor at the rear of the saloon and French Dinky Toys offered it as a model, thus spreading its fame among young enthusiasts. There were both suburban and city versions of this design, the former (201 in total, 65 passengers) having all-metal bodies by Million-Guiet-Tubauto, the latter (100, 55 passengers) composite bodies built in the undertaking's own workshops. This design performed well and remained in service until 1971.

In 1953 there was a reversion to Chausson, with the purchase of 60 basically similar buses of type APH 2.52 (75-124 and 275-284). There was still a good deal of the coach about this design, in particular in the low roof, and the last ten, which were to be used on private hire and sightseeing duties, were given small windows in the roof. The following Chausson design was much more of a bus. This was type APU 53, of which, according to RATP records, there were ultimately 273 (1001-1273) in the fleet. However, the number 1001 was later used on a Somua OP5-3 (qv) and it may be that the numbers of class APU53 ran from 1002 to 1274. Unlike all previous buses bought from this manufacturer, these were designed for urban operation and had double-width rear and central doors and a single-width door at the front. Again small roof

BELOW: No 3158 has been cosmetically restored to its war time condition with gas-bag and is seen in the centenary exhibition at La Villette in October 2006. *(Author)*

ABOVE: Chausson 1234 is working on line 22 at Concorde in April 1968. (Author)

RIGHT: Chausson APU 5 no.1090 working on trolleybus replacement line 163 at Porte de Champerret c1965. (J-B Prudhommeaux, collection Assa)

BELOW: Chausson 1267 has just begun its journey back to the Gare de l'Est and is on the Right Bank opposite the Eiffel Tower on 15th August 1970. (Julian Osborne)

lights were provided, this time in the interests of standing passengers. A conductor was carried and had a post at the rear, passengers leaving by the middle and front doors. These also lasted until 1971. Finally between 1956 and 1965 no fewer than 756 Chausson buses of type APVU were acquired, in six discrete batches. This model was higher than its predecessors and therefore the roof lights had to go. Series 1 and Series 2 vehicles, delivered between 1956 and 1959, were laid out for driver-only operation, for 65 passengers. These numbered 174 in total. Series 3 (1960) and Series 5 (1962) buses had conductors and could accommodate 75 passengers. There were 72 of these. The most numerous type, with 410 examples, was Series 4, also of 1962, which were again designed for one-man operation and could carry 65. Fleet numbers were 130-277, 1275-1400 and 1740-2212, but it is not now

ABOVE: Somua three-door model 339 is seen on line 42 on the left bank near the Eiffel Tower in April 1968. *(Author)*

RIGHT: Somua two-door OP5/2 749 is on the Avenue de Nogent in the Bois de Vincennes about 1966. *(J-B Prudhommeaux, collection Assa)*

BELOW RIGHT: The class leader of the last batch of Somua buses to be delivered, 1501, is at Porte d'Auteuil terminus of suburban line 123, in the late 1960s. *(J B Prudhommeaux, collection Assa)*

possible to decide which type carried which numbers. All the Chaussons lasted until the early 1970s.

In 1955 a further series of Somua buses arrived, with type OP5-3. This design was based closely on the OP5, but was slightly longer and had a central door in addition to those at rear and front. In all there were 380 of this class (321-500 and 802-1001). A further 240 (1501-1740, class OP 5-3 SB3) appeared in 1960. These lacked the roof number box of the earlier designs. All were bodied by Million-Guet and the last few carried the Saviem badge, Somua having amalgamated with Renualt and Latil to form this new concern. The last OP5-3 was withdrawn in 1974.

Also in 1955 the manufacturer Berliet of Lyon managed for the first time (apart from a single prototype) to break into the Paris market, with a batch of 100 of type PCP10 (1401-1500), delivered in 1955. As 80 of these were bodied by MGT, it is not surprising that they resembled the contemporary Somua design. The other 20 were given bodies by CIV. In service they were noisy and were not as well-liked as the Somuas, being prone to vibration. In 1960 an improved version, classified PCS10 appeared and there were 50 of these (1-50) and the last five to be built had parabolic windscreens, anticipating those fitted to the later Standard buses. The last of the Berliets ran in 1972.

There was then a lull in new construction for some years, apart from the appearance in 1961 of a series of 60 minibuses (4501-4560), built by Verney, type RU. These were built as an experiment, to try to woo motorists out of their cars by the provision of a high frequency service, using smaller and more manoeuvrable buses. A flat fare was charged – at that time Paris buses had a stage fare structure – and, as a special attraction, smoking was permitted on board. Two lines were operated ; line A ran between Bourse and Porte Maillot and line B between Invalides and Place Clichy. To

LEFT: C53 Berliet PCS10 20 is also at Porte d'Auteuil on line 123, but with the trees of the Bois de Boulogne in the background. As with the Somuas delivered in the same year, these buses could be distinguished by the lack of a roof number box. This change marked a break with a tradition going back to the Schneider P2s of 1911. *(J-B Prudhommeaux, collection Assa)*

BELOW LEFT: C54 Berliet PCP10 no.1440 at Châtillon in the south of the city. It is performing a short working of line 68, this being denoted by the red diagonal bar across the number. *(J-B Prudhommeaux, collection Assa)*

distinguish these from the normal service buses, the minibuses were given an attractive livery of light blue and cream. The experiment was certainly successful in attracting traffic, to the extent where the minibuses had to be replaced by full-size vehicles and the lines became 46, 82 and (in part) 303 in 1965. The minibuses were then used for some years on other services.

In 1964 a Leyland Atlantean with Alexander-style bodywork was imported and run on the routes of various services, but it had not been adapted for right-hand traffic and so did not carry passengers. The experiment had no immediate result.

Despite the influx of new vehicles in the 1950s, the condition of the bus fleet in the early 1960s was still not altogether satisfactory. The pre-war buses were at last reaching the end of their useful lives and there were three quite different types of post-war units in service, of which the earlier Chaussons were not really suitable for urban work. This variety, while interesting to the enthusiast, required a multiplicity of spare parts and increased considerably the work of the maintenance staff.

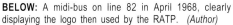

BELOW: A midi-bus on line 82 in April 1968, clearly displaying the logo then used by the RATP. *(Author)*

The 'Standards'
Saviem SC10 and
Berliet PCM-R

Studies of a standard design began in 1955, in co-operation with UTPUR (Union des Transports Publiques Urbains et Régionaux), since it was hoped that provincial operators would also show interest in the concept. It was then decided to seek tenders for a standard bus, of dimensions approximately 10m x 2.5m, from various manufacturers and on 5th July 1962 three prototypes, from three manufacturers, were presented to the Minister of Public Works. The firms which accepted the challenge of meeting the demanding specifications were Saviem, Verney and Berliet. All buses were 11m long, with three doorways and parabolic windscreens. The height of the floor above road level was reduced compared to that on earlier designs and the step height at the doors was also reduced, both these features allowing quicker boarding and alighting. However, due to the low floor height, seats had to be mounted 140mm above that of the central gangway. Seats could be either in facing pairs or all facing the direction of travel. The Berliet (4451) and Saviem (4450) vehicles were designed for two-person operation, with three doors and a conductor's post between the rear and middle doors. That by Verney (4452) was intended for driver-only operation on outer-suburban services and the single-width rear door was for emergency use only. Both seating and standing capacities varied (see table) and each bus had a slightly different interior layout, with different decor. All, however, had fluorescent lighting. Exterior paint schemes also varied and the Saviem caused something of an outcry by appearing in a red livery. This was an idea

TOP RIGHT: One of the three-door city buses, 5398, with single-width front door, as delivered, approaching Place de la Concorde in April 1968. *(Author)*

CENTRE RIGHT: After conversion to driver-only operation, the front door was made double-width, as seen on 7748, on a short working of line 95 in June 1982 *(Author)*

RIGHT: Driver-only operated 5149 is seen at Porte de la Chapelle – Saint-Gratien on line 256. *(AMTUIR, collection Assa)*

of M. Weil, intended to distinguish suburban buses from those on city service, but it was heavily criticised and lasted for a very short time only. From the driver's point of view, the most significant development was that of a standardised driving position, no matter the make of bus. Engines were by MAN (Berliet), Saviem (Saviem) and Hispano. The prototypes went on to become trainers.

After trials in service, orders were placed with Saviem and Berliet. Although the Verney prototype had performed equally well, that firm did not have the capacity to meet orders for a large number of buses. Operation began in the suburbs in October 1965, with vehicles for driver-only operation being painted in the unpopular red livery. They were repainted green in the following year. The buses built by Saviem were classified SC10 U and 300 (5101-5400) formed the initial order. Of these, the first 40 wore the red livery. The first Saviems for conductor operation went into service on line 72 (Saint-Cloud – Hôtel de Ville) in April 1966, followed soon afterwards by the first Berliets on line 30 (Trocadéro – Gare de l'Est). Deliveries continued until 1979, by which year no fewer than 2,190 were in service, a record for a single type of vehicle in Paris. The Saviems were of chassisless construction, while the buses built by Berliet had separate chassis and bodywork. However, all the bodies looked identical to the casual observer and came in three varieties – city buses with three doors, suburban buses for conductor operation, also having three doors and suburban buses for driver-only operation with front and centre doors and, on the first deliveries, an outward-opening door at the rear. This feature was not perpetuated. The first order for the Berliet PCM-R design was for 300 and later orders took this total to 750, only 121 of these being for use within Paris. These were numbered 4151-4500 and 4601-5000. This firm withdrew from production of the standard bus in 1972, in favour of its own designs. All standard buses had MAN engines.

With increased comfort for both passengers and crews, the standard buses were an instant success and for almost forty years were a typical part of the city's street scene. As the design was produced over such a long period, it was natural that there should be some alterations to take account of the changing needs of passengers and, beginning with no.7291 of 1975 (7291-7335), a more comfortable and spacious interior was provided, at the expense of several seats. There were now only 35 of these and this caused some complaints, since traffic had just begun to increase with the introduction of the Carte Orange. In the next year's delivery (7336-7475) seating was increased

29

LEFT: When withdrawn, many Standards have become works vehicles, one of which participated in the centenary procession in 2006. It is seen awaiting departure at the Petit Palais. *(Author)*
BELOW LEFT: Double-decker 2212 crosses the Pont de la Concorde in April 1974. The National Assembly is in the background. *(Author)*

to 37 by the expedient of fitting back-to-back seats over the wheel arches. These were classified SC10 U M *(modernisé)*. For the Ceinture service, a different interior layout was developed with only 33 seats and an enlarged standing area by the centre doors (7486-7585, SC10 U M 2C). In 1977, for suburban routes, 200 buses (7656-7855, SC10 U M 2R) were delivered with "rotonde" (perimeter) seating and an enlarged standing area, for 47 passengers. This arrangement was continued on other buses intended for use on suburban lines (7901-9050, SC10 U M 2CR). Another variant was type SC 10 U-X (6000-6100), which had higher speed engines and were used mainly on lines which ran for part of their route on motorway.

Berliet double-deck PCM-RE

There were only three external variations in design during the period over which these buses were built. In 1966 the prototype (2200) of a double-deck design appeared from Berliet, classified PCM-RE (E - étage) and what was intended to be a first series of 25 was ordered in June of that year (2201-2225). This design was based closely on the standard single-deck design but was rather shorter. It has been said that this was the brain-child of a particular Prefect of Police and that, when he retired from office, no one else had any interest in them and they were withdrawn at what was for a Paris bus, a relatively young age. Headroom in both saloons was generous, being 1.85m in the lower saloon and 1.73m on the upper deck. The prototype had a single-width front doorway and double-width centre and rear doors, but on the production series, the single-width door was in the centre. There were two rearward-ascending staircases and originally the conductor had a fixed post at the rear of the lower saloon, just at the foot of the rear stair. In due course, when they were converted for driver-only operation, passenger flow was reversed. In service they proved to be a disappointment. While the upper deck provided a good vantage point for sightseeing, many passengers were reluctant to climb up to it for what was in most cases, a fairly short journey. In the event, the 'first' series was the only one. The double-deckers spent most of their lives on lines 53 (Opéra–Pont d'Asnières) and 94 (Montparnasse–Mairie de Levallois), being withdrawn in 1977/8. Some then became mobile blood-donor centres and one has been preserved.

Berliet PGR short 'standard'

The second variation from the standard design appeared in 1968, when Berliet delivered the first of type PGR – petit gabarit or what would now in Britain be termed a midibus. These were shorter and narrower than the standard single-decker and had only front and centre doors, being one-person operated from the start. They were intended for use on lines traversing narrow streets and it was hoped that they would be able to increase the speed of service on such streets. In practice, the reduced dimensions made virtually no difference to their average speed and they were too small to cope with the increase in ridership which came in the mid-1970s. There were originally 560 buses of this type (2441-3000), placed in service between 1968 and 1971, but by 1979 only 141 remained in service and all had gone soon afterwards. An even smaller design, in the form of a Citroen minibus, was tried in 1972, when 18 (101-118) were bought to provide a service in the Bois de Boulogne, but this lasted only until 1979 and when it was withdrawn, the minibuses migrated to the suburbs.

LEFT: One of the PGR buses, 2786, awaits departure from Hôtel de Ville for Vanves in June 1982. *(Author)*

Open platform

A milestone in the history of the Paris bus, regretted by Parisians and visitors alike, was the disappearance of the open-platform design on 22nd January 1971, when the last of the type made its final journey on line 21, Saint-Lazare–Porte de Gentilly. Many people made their views about this known to the RATP. When Saviem SC10 no.5933 arrived at the central workshop one day in 1975, following rear-end damage in an accident, it occurred to the staff that it could be repaired in such a way as to provide an open rear platform and they received agreement to proceed with the idea. When the bus re-entered service, it proved to be so popular that ten similar, new vehicles (7476-7485) were ordered in 1976 and 45 (7856-7900) more followed in the next year. When a restyled version of the standard class appeared, 35 were built to open platform layout (SC10 RA), the last of such buses to be delivered to the RATP. The platform, which could accommodate ten standees, was, of course, not used by boarding passengers, who entered at the front in the by-now usual way. A sliding door, operated by a push-button separated it from the saloon. It was simply an observation area, from which one had a wonderful view of all that was going on in the city streets. These buses operated on lines which served areas frequented by tourists, such as line 20 between the Gare de Lyon and the Gare St-Lazare via the Grands Boulevards, and proved to be extremely popular. There was great sorrow when they were withdrawn at the turn of the millennium and, as it was not possible to repeat the design with current

TOP: One of the open platform buses of the first type, 7865, working on line 20. *(Author)*
ABOVE: Open-platform 3976, wearing the corporate livery introduced in 1992, awaits the start of the centenary parade in Avenue Winston Churchill on 15th October 2006. *(Author)*

standard buses, it is likely that these will be the last open-platform buses to run in Paris. Several have been preserved.

As with the main design, this type was also operated in provincial cities.

LEFT: One of the later type, 3954, at Château de Vincennes on 19th July 2000. *(Author)*

ABOVE: Standard 8431 at the junction of rue La Fayette and rue de Dunkirque, passing the Picardy Hotel, whilst heading for Gare du Nord on line 42 in August 1986. *(Mike Davis)*

BELOW: Seen here near Place Clichy is another Standard, 8849, whilst running over the granite sette road surface still common in 1980s Paris. It is en route to Republique on line 54, again in August 1986. *(Mike Davis)*

SC10R *(restylé)*

By 1980, all earlier types had been retired and there were 3,900 standard buses in service. However, the first of these were beginning to show their age. As the design had proved to give every satisfaction, it was decided that a cosmetic change would be all that was required in replacement buses and accordingly Saviem produced a bus with a new design of front end and internal improvements. Designated SC 10 R *(Restylé)*, this type first appeared in 1981 and between that year and 1988, 1,598 were built (including 35 with open platform). Numbers were 9351-9999 and 3001-3947. The last ran on 12th March 2002 and in total over 5,000 buses based on the standard concept ran in Paris in almost 40 years.

ABOVE: Seen on the same day in August 1986, and in the same location, as Standard 8431 on a previous page, Renault-badged Saviem SC10R, No 3343 is also approaching Gare du Nord, but on line 46 from Vincennes. *(Mike Davis)*

BELOW: Saviem SC10R No 3946 at Gare de Lyon in August 2000, en route for Porte de la Muette. *(Author)*

Airport buses

In 1974 new services were inaugurated by the RATP to serve the city's airports of Orly (from Denfert-Rocherau) and Roissy Charles de Gaulle (from Gare de l'Est). Twenty new rear-engined buses were bought to work on these lines. For use on line 215 to Orly, there were ten Saviem E 110 vehicles (5001-5010), while for line 350 to Roissy, 20 Berliet PR 100 vehicles (4001-4020) were acquired. Both types had a good deal of the coach about them and were the first rear-engined buses to be used in regular service by the RATP. The Berliets were fitted with Perkins engines, which proved to be noisy and unreliable and had to be replaced by the builder's own engines in 1977. The Berliet design was then developed into the PR 100 M1, originally intended for urban use, but later transferred to suburban operation and used particularly on lines which made use of motorways, on which their high speed capabilities could be used to the full. Between 1987 and 1993 all these were replaced by Berliet PR100-2 buses, which were in turn withdrawn in 2001/2.

Experimental buses

After the fuel crisis of 1973, there was some interest in finding other sources of fuel for the buses and in 1974 and again in 1978 the RATP, in co-operation with Gaz de France and Saviem, experimented with buses using gas rather than diesel. In the first case, the gas used was natural liquified gas, while in the second it was liquified petroleum gas.

There was no immediate outcome of these tests. Nor did the demonstration in 1977 of four rear-engined buses built by foreign manufacturers – Mercedes-Benz (501), Scania (502), Volvo (503) and Magirus-Deutz (504) – result in any change in policy when new buses were acquired in the 1980s.

Two Heuliez buses were purchased in 1986. They were both sold for further service in 1995

BELOW LEFT: The Volvo experimental bus was numbered 503 by RATP. *(DTS Collection)*

BELOW RIGHT: 504, the Magirus-Deutz. *(DTS Collection)*

Renault PR100 and PR180

The growth in passenger numbers from 1975 onwards convinced RATP managers that on some lines there was now a need for buses of a higher capacity. On 30th April 1983 there appeared the first articulated bus, marketed as "Superbus" and used on line 19 (Gare Montparnasse – Bastille), on which over 40,000 passengers were carried daily. This design was now built by Renault as type PR180; 44 were destined for urban service an eleven for airport service to Orly.

A second batch followed (PR180-2), some of which were used on the Trans Val-deMarne busway and for this they received a blue and white livery. They were successful in service, there being ultimately 326 of this type, and lasted until 2003. On articulated buses, all doors were then used for both entry and exit. None of these is now in service, all having been replaced by Agora L vehicles.

Citroen sold Berliet to Renault in 1976 but until 1980 the two badges – Saviem and Berliet – were continued. In 1980 Renault replaced both. So the 1977 PR100MI was launched under Renault's auspices.

LEFT: PR100MI, 4090, from the first series of this type to be badged Renault. *(Malcolm Chase)*

BELOW: Preserved Renault PR100.2, 4199, in the Centre Bus de Montrouge during an open day on 20th September 2008. *(Author)*

ABOVE: The articulated version of the PR100 was designated the PR180: an example is seen here leaving Gare Montparnasse on 27th April 1996. *(Julian Osborne)*

RIGHT: PR180 4626, outward bound to Ivry on line 27, swings into a bend at Palais Royal in May 1984. *(Author)*

Trolleybuses

Paris was one of the first European cities to experiment with this form of transport.

In 1900 a Lombard-Guérin "electrobus" ran between Porte de Vincennes, Saint-Mandé and Lac Daumesnil during the exposition of that year. This was an improved version of the vehicle demonstrated by Siemens in Berlin in the previous year, having been adapted by two Parisian engineers, Lombard and Guérin. There were twin lines of overhead, from which current was collected by a small four-wheel chariot, connected to the bus by a flexible cable. The line served the pavilions devoted to agriculture and service ceased when the exposition closed. It is not known what happened to the vehicles. Another electric bus was tried in Saint-Mandé in 1912, but this was not a trolleybus.

Based on conversions from Schneider H type motorbuses (173, 228 and 1266), three trolleybuses were tried by the STCRP in January 1922 on the suburban tram line between Enghien and Montmorency. Another experiment, using the same vehicles, took place in Vitry in 1925 but there was no permanent outcome of either of these trials. Nonetheless, these were followed in 1929 by trials, also at Vitry, of using two Renaults of type PY (4001/2). Problems with the electric motors increased with age and the service was converted to motorbus operation in 1935. In 1936 TN 6C 2728 was converted into a petrol-electric trolleybus, retaining its petrol engine with the electric motors suspended below the bodywork. It is not clear where this operated and again these trials had no permanent result.

It was not until the second world war that modern trolleybuses began to run in Paris. The lack of fuel for motor buses suggested that this would be a good time to install these and this co-incided with the internal politics of the newly-merged organisation of STCRP and CMP. The most convinced advocate of the trolleybus was Jean Berthelot, one of the chief engineers of the new organisation and a close colleague of Marshal Pétain, now head of state.

Vetra CS 60

A fleet of 40 two-axle Vetra CS 60 (8001-8040) vehicles was ordered on 27th August 1940, but these were not delivered until 1942 and it was not until 1943 that lines 63 and 64, running from Porte de Champerret into the north-west suburbs, were converted for operation by trolleybuses. These vehicles were definitely on the small side and could carry only 50 passengers. However, they did introduce passenger flow to the capital's transport and also brought the comfort of a totally-enclosed body. The rear entrance and forward exit were enclosed by folding doors and the conductor had a fixed post just ahead of the rear door. A small Peugeot engine, mounted at the rear, allowed the buses to manoeuvre away from the overhead wires. Service on line 63 began on 8 January 1943 and on line 64 on 6 September of the same year. These Vetras ran until 1956, although some of this class were removed to Germany, where they ended up in Silesia and did not return to Paris after 1945. The two services, which in the meantime had become 163 and 164, were converted to diesel operation on 1st January 1960 and 1st April 1962 respectively.

Vetra VBRh

In 1948 and 1950 two further lines were opened in the south-east of the city, line 183 from Porte de Choisy to Choisy-le-Roi and line 185 from Porte d'Italie to Thiais. Once again Vetra supplied the vehicles, this time 55 of type VBRh (8051-8105), which were rather larger and more powerful than the CS 60s, but like them had an auxiliary motor. They also operated on lines 163 and 164. Vehicles for the two new services were shedded at Ivry. These latter trolleybuses ran until all services ceased on 1st April 1966 and 24 were then sold for further service in Limoges, where they remained in service until the late 1980s.

Vetra VBF

To replace the original vehicles, 38 Vetra VBF vehicles (8106-8143) were bought in 1957. They were slightly larger than the VBR type and, in common with contemporary motorbuses, had three doors. All were sold to Grenoble after the closure of the Paris system and were renumbered 629-666 (not in sequence).

Demonstrators

These had some influence on the design of the Standard motorbus. Around 1950 several vehicles built by various manufacturers for provincial systems were briefly tried in Paris but none were acquired. There was also an unusual four-axle articulated vehicle built for Algiers, essentially a three-axle chassis with a trailing two-axle section, but it did not find any favour with the RATP.

ABOVE LEFT: Vetra CS 8032 at Porte de Champerret in 1951. Cross-platform interchange was provided with bus line PC at this point. *(Jacques Bazin, collection Assa)*

LEFT: VBRh 8089 at Porte de Champerret on line 163 in 1951. *(Jacques Bazin, collection Assa)*

LEFT: This 1963 view of 8125, depicts a Vetra type VBF, the final series of Paris trolleybuses, all of which were subsequently transferred to Grenoble. *(Peter Shearman)*

The Present Fleet

Renault R 312

Good though the standard design was, it clearly could not last for ever, and as early as 1979 studies were set on foot to determine the basic parameters of "*l'Autobus Futur*", also known as GG79-85. Heuliez produced the outline of this concept, of which a mock-up was shown to officials and operators in December 1979. This bus had a horizozntal rear engine, a lower floor level than previous designs and a flat floor throughout. The seats were cantilevered out from the sides of the body. The original specification was revised and a full-size mock-up was produced by Renault in 1981. Four prototype and nine pre-production vehicles were commissioned, and RATP was entrusted with designing various aspects of the new bus, as well as fitting-out the body shells of the pre-production vehicles. The first of these, RATP 5001, entered experimental service in early 1985, on line 21, (Gare Saint-Lazare – Porte de Gentilly). Two more buses (5002/3) joined it, and the other six went to Toulouse, Strasbourg, Angoulême, Le Havre, Marseille and Lyon. Quantity production of what had become the vertically rear-engined R312 began in 1988, after extensive trials with the pre-production batch.

5001 was joined on 17th February 1986 by 5003. These two had different interior and exterior colour schemes and no.5001 was christened the "*Boîte à petit pois*" (Tin of peas), as its exterior was liberally sprinkled with little green dots. 5002 was used for experiments with hydrostatic transmission and did not enter passenger service.

The first production R312 went into service on line 38 on 1st June 1988. It had a rather drab external livery of white and black, with a thin pale green band. The first batches (nos.5011 to 5948, a total of 938), delivered up to 1993, had three doors, greatly improving passenger flow and in the early 1990s some were fitted with external passenger door control, as part of an experiment to assess the possibility of using all doors for both entry and exit. They ran only on lines 28 and 38, but fraud increased and the experiment was abandoned in 1995.

Deliveries from that year onwards (5949-6604) were fitted with only two doors, the central door being moved by one bay to the rear of the bus, to improve internal circulation. These brought the total of this type to 1,594, and all were painted in the new RATP livery of jade green and white.

This class is now in course of withdrawal and all should be gone by 2010.

ABOVE LEFT: 1587 shows the three-door layout, as it leaves the terminus of line 93 at Esplanade des Invalides, Air France terminal, on 16th April 2008. This building was originally a station and was opened in 1900, when the Chemins de Fer de l'Ouest extended its line inwards to this point. *(Author)*

LEFT: 6201 is one of the later two-door models, seen at Château de Vincennes bus station on the same date. The difference in height compared to Agora 2080 on the left can be appreciated. *(Author)*

Renault Agora

As had happened in the past, a number of buses were bought from various manufacturers for evaluation against the 'standard' bus, which was now the R312. The first, 505, was new c1990 and was on a Van Hool chassis. The second, 506 was a prototype Setra S300NC, new in 1992, which in 1997 became 3019 in the fleet of Transpole, Lille. The third, 507, was an early Mercedes O405N, also new in 1992, and which had gone to TRAM, Mulhouse by mid-1994. 506/7 were both three-door vehicles. Partly as a result, the Renault R312 design was further developed into the Renault Agora, which appeared in December 1996 and was the first low floor bus to run in Paris. There were 115 of this type. The floor height was only 32cm above road level and there were no intermediate steps, but there was no ramp for wheelchairs and the bus could not kneel at stops to allow passengers with reduced mobility to board. The RATP thought that a gradient of 16% could safely be negotiated by a person in a wheelchair, without the necessity for lowering the bus. However, this idea was not well received by the organisations representing wheelchair users and it was realised that features to address their concerns would be necessary on all new deliveries. There was a slight pause in deliveries until the concept was refined. Deliveries of what was now classified Agora V 2 then ran from 1999 to 2001, there being a total of 1,222 buses of this variety. They were followed by the basically similar Agora Line, of which there are 419 in service. Operators were now becoming increasingly aware of the need to combat pollution and in 1999 a variation of the Agora – Agora GNV (*gaz naturel pour véhicules* = natural gas for vehicles) – appeared on the streets, the first gas-powered bus to run in passenger service since the second world war. This design used natural gas, with an improved form of combustion to the buses of the 1940s, and carrying the fuel in a streamlined tank mounted on the front part of the roof. This contains nine reservoirs, with a total capacity of 1134 litres. A rainbow-coloured band above the front saloon windows proudly proclaims the type's green credentials. Fifty-three of these (7201-7253) were placed in service from Créteil garage between June 1999 and April 2001. These were the first RATP buses to be bought following European-wide tendering.

The Agora design was also expanded into an articulated vehicle, Agora-L (long), which first appeared in June 1997 and which was delivered until October 2001. There are 438 of these and they are used on the busiest services such as the PC lines and the services using the Val-de-Marne busway, for which they have received a special livery. Some of these buses are air conditioned. Numbers are 1501-1650, 1701-1809 and 4401-4579.

ABOVE: Renault Agora 7210 working on line 26 at Saint-Lazare in November 2005. The coloured discs along the waistband remind passengers that boarding is by the front door only. *(Author)*

ABOVE RIGHT: Agora no.7043, using Liquid Petroleum Gas power, at Saint-Lazare in November 2005. *(Author)*

RIGHT: Agora L 1745 at Porte de Choisy terminus of line 183 in March 2007. This line, once a trolleybus service, is one of the busiest on the road network and at peak periods requires a three-minute frequency, all with articulated vehicles. In the near future, the outer portion will be replaced by a tram line. *(Author)*

BELOW: Agora 2080 is one of the early deliveries and has the middle door placed further forward than on subsequent vehicles. It is leaving the bus station at Château de Vincennes on 16th April 2008. *(Author)*

BELOW RIGHT: Irisbus Agora 8392 at Denfert-Rocherau on line 68 on 16th April 2008. *(Author)*

Heuliez GX 317

There was also increasing pressure from politicians and the group (COLITRAH) representing people with mobility impairment to operate buses which would be completely accessible. When Renault announced that they were not themselves willing to produce a low floor vehicle which would meet these conditions, RATP then agreed to take a series of such buses which would be bodied by the firm of Heuliez as sub-contractors. The first of their products to appear was the GX 317, which was fitted with a lowering mechanism and a ramp, to allow wheelchair users to board at stops. These went into service on line 20 in 1995/6 and numbers reached 124 (1001-1124), though only those of the first batch are fully accessible. Externally these are almost identical to the basic Agora design and like it, were followed in 1999 by a version running on liquid petroleum gas (GX 317 GPL). There are 57 of these (8001-8057), garaged at Aubervilliers. The two reservoirs on the roof contain 300 litres of gas and allow a range of 400km between re-fuelling.

ABOVE LEFT: Heuliez 1086 working on outer-suburban line 388 at Châtillon-Montrouge station on 20th September 2008. The Métro is on the viaduct behind. *(Author)*

ABOVE RIGHT: One of the Heuliez buses running on LPG, 8050, at Rond-Point des Champs-Elysées on 16th April 2008. *(Author)*

Mercedes-Benz Citaro Evobus

ABOVE: Citaro 4307 at Gare de l'Est on the service to Roissy on 9th April 2008. The memory of the former tram terminus at this point is kept alive by the name of the bistro behind the bus. (Author)

The products of foreign manufacturers have also appeared in RATP service. The Mercedes-Benz Citaro Evobus arrived in 2001/2 when 70 buses of this type (4251-4320) went into service on outer suburban lines, to replace the Renault PR100. Air conditioning is fitted. Originally these buses had engines conforming to Euro 2 norms but these have now been replaced by the model meeting Euro 3 norms. As a sign of the times, these buses also have a screen to protect the driver from assault. These are the first non-French vehicles to be acquired since the NAG double-deck prototype in 1905. Two have since been lost due to fire damage.

Scania Omnicity-L

From October 2002, there were delivered eleven Scania Omnicity-L articulated vehicles (1681-1691) which are used on airport services. These have an enhanced level of comfort and a capability of running at 90km/hr, although this speed is not attained in normal service. As these had proved successful, RATP then ordered 125 Omnicity-S two-axle vehicles in the autumn of 2005, with an option for a further 175. The first entered service on line 143 in March 2007

RIGHT: Scania articulated 1691 awaits airport passengers at Denfert-Rochereau on 16th April 2008. *(Author)*

BELOW: Scania S 9358 on Avenue Franklin D Roosevelt at Rond-Point des Champs-Elysées on 16th April 2008. *(Author)*

MAN NL223

The Scanias were followed in 2003/4 by no fewer than 180 buses of type NL223 from MAN in Germany and these have proved to be popular with passengers, no doubt because of their improved level of comfort compared to the Agora. A further order took the total to 205 (9001-9205). The first went into service on line 28, but they are now in widespread use on the urban system. To replace articulated Agora buses, which had been transferred from line 183 to reinforce the fleet in service on the TVM busway (*page 13 and 38*), an articulated version of this bus, the MAN NG, was also bought and there are now 15 of these in the fleet (4601-4615).

ABOVE RIGHT: MAN NL223 9010 picking up passengers at Rond-Pont de Champs-Elysées on 16th April 2008. *(Author)*

RIGHT: MAN artic. 4615 is outbound on line 183 on the busway on the Boulevard de Stalingrad at Vitry on 21th September 2008. The bellows above the articulation is made of translucent material, to give a brighter interior. The Centre Bus de Vitry is the white building on the left. *(Author)*

Irisbus Citélis Line

Finally, to accelerate the programme to make all vehicles accessible to all passengers, RATP ordered 365 Citélis Line buses from Iveco in 2005. These have a brighter and more "environmental" interior decor, with much use of light colours. The first entered service in late 2006, on what remained of line PC1 after most of this had been converted to tram operation. By January 2008 220 were in service and their use is steadily being expanded.

Fleet numbers are 3001-3365. There is an option for 506 further vehicles of this type. This design can easily be adapted to work with an optical guidance system.

ABOVE: Citélis 3166 turns from Avenue Ledru-Rollin into rue de Charonne on line 76 on 17th April 2008. *(Author)*

The Current and Future RATP fleet

As of October 2007 RATP had a fleet of 4227 buses, of which the Agora in its various forms accounted for over half the total. RATP placed orders for 356 articulated buses in 2008 (186 Lion's City buses from MAN and 170 Citélis-18s. Of the MANs, 170 will be 18m long with 44 seats and the others will be 18.75m long, with 56 seats, for use on Roissybus airport service 352. The articulation joints will be of translucent material). Some of the future deliveries will probably be built as Créalis, a designer version of the Citélis.

BELOW: As mentioned in the introduction, some services in the outer suburbs are provided by private operators, using their own vehicles, which are painted in RATP corporate livery. In this view a Renault PR112, operated by TRA and numbered 46663, is seen at Parc des Expositions, near Roissy airport, in November 2005. *(Author)*

Mini- and Midibuses

During the last forty years RATP has experimented with smaller buses of various types, some of which have had rather brief lives. Between 1972 and 1975 18 Citroën Currus minibuses were purchased for use on services within La Défense and in the Bois de Boulogne. These services were withdrawn in 1979 and the buses ended their days working in the eastern suburbs and in Boulogne-Billancourt. Six Saviem SB 2 vehicles (119-124) were bought for a dial-a-bus service in Saint-Cloud, which ran from 1975 to 1982. In February 1983 some

Heuliez minibuses introduced the Montmartrobus service but were quickly superseded some CBM220 midibuses. After trials with a Belgian Van Hool AU138 midibus, numbered 701, eight similar A508 buses (711-718) were bought for use on this service and later battery buses, beginning with Gruau MG36s, 301/2, were used on it. In mid-1998 two Renault R212 buses were bought from Auto Nice Transport for use on local services at Rosny and Fontenay-sous-Bois, which the local councils had asked RATP to provide. It was most unusual for RATP to buy second-hand vehicles, but at the time it had no suitable small buses, having sold the last CBM 220s a couple of years earlier. These buses were equipped with air conditioning and had previously been used on Nice Airport shuttles. They had been withdrawn by 2003. At present a total of 138 small buses is in service on a variety of lines, most of which either serve suburban communities, often in conjunction with the local authority, or, within Paris, run in areas which are not open to full-size vehicles. Full details are given in the fleet list.

LEFT: CBM No 613 was one of a small fleet of midibuses introduced on the 'Montmartrobus' service from 1983 and is seen here in Montmartre in August 1986. There were altogether 18 CBM220 midibuses for the 'Montmartrobus' service. They were numbered 601-618 and built between 1983 and 1986. All were initially 25 seaters but 602 and 606 were later reduced to 21 to make wheelchair space at the rear. Withdrawals took place between 1991 and 1996, and several examples have gone for further service. (Mike Davis)

RIGHT: Heuliez GX77 654 at the Utrillo stop by the Sacré Coeur in Montmartre on 14th October 2006. (Author)

BELOW: Gruau microbus 729 at Gambetta, terminus of the Traverse de Charonne service, on 14th October 2006. (Author)

BELOW RIGHT: A later version of Montmartrobus. 711-8 were integral Van Hool A508-MANs, all new in February-March 1990, and were 22-seaters. They were mainly withdrawn in 2004 (711, however, went in 2000). No 716, ascends the long hill to the Place du Tertre terminus. (Ron Phillips)

Technical details of main classes

Type	Length	Width	Height	Weight	Engine	Capacity
P2	6.24m	2.19m	4.25m	6.5t	35hp	16/14+2
Schneider PB2	7.56m	2.30m	3.10m	5.4t	35hp	28+7
De Dion Bouton	6.91m	2.19m	?	5.07t	30hp	31
Schneider H	8.38m	2.19m	3.07m	5.2t	30hp	28+10
Schneider H6	10.43m	2.19m	3.07m	7t	30hp	40+8
Renault PN	8.19m	2.37m	2.88m	5.62t	45hp	28+12
TN 4 A1	9.19m	2.41m	2.97m	6.11t	58hp	33+17
TN 4 A2	9.19m	2.41m	2.97m	6.11t	58hp	33+17
TN 6 A2	9.50m	2.41m	2.97m	7.1t	67hp	33+17
TN4H (Paris)	9.76m	2.35m	3.11m	7.400kg	58hp	41+9
(The Panhard K 63 was identical)						
Somua OP5	10.20m	2.50m	2.86m	11.9t	100hp	31+34
Somua OP5-3	10.61m	2.49m	2.85m	8.845kg	120hp	33+22 (Paris), 29+36 (suburban)
Chauss.APH2-52	10.18m	2.50m	2.88m	7.64t	80hp	43+26
Chausson APVU	10.32m	2.50m	2.98m	8.750kg	120hp	44+21 (Grande banlieue)
Berliet PCP10	10.82m	2.46m	2.86m	8.77t	145hp	29+36
Verney midibus	7.46m	2.45m	2.68m	5.210kg	80hp	20+12
Saviem SC10 U	11.00m	2.50m	2.94m	8.,160kg	135hp	30+52 (Paris), 23+64 (suburban) 36+42 (Grande banlieue)
Berliet PCM-RE	9.83m	2.50m	4.35m	9.5t	135hp	54+30 (Double-deck)
Citroen minibus	5.34m	2.04m	2.24m	2.0t	11hp	13+0
Berliet PR100	11.35m	2.50m	2.94m	9.1t	180hp	38+32
Berliet PR 180	17.54m	2.50m	2.96m	?	225hp	?
Berliet PGR	9.00m	2.25m	2.99m	6.76t	112hp	28+17
Saviem SC10UA	11.00m	2.50m	2.94m	8.25t	144hp	38+30 (Open platform)
Renault SC10 R	11.00m	2.50m	2.94m	8.2t	144hp	33+45 (Restyled)
Renault PR180-2	17.67m	2.50m	3.05m	16.5t	253ho	35+105 (articulated)
Renault R 312	11.90m	2.50m	3.09m	11.62t	206hp	31+77 (three-door layout)
Renault Agora	11.99m	2.5m	2.93m	11.64t	206hp	27+67 (two-door layout)
Renault Agora L	17.80m	2.50m	2.93m	17.3t	253hp	37+117 (articulated)
Heuliez GX 317	11.99m	2.5m	2.92m	11.56t	206hp	28+89 (two-door version)
Oreso 55E	7.71m	2.22m	3.03m	9.35t	120hp	17 (4 strapontins) +33
Scania artic.	17.99m	2.50m	2.97m	16.1t	260hp	55+77
MAN NL223	11.95m	2.50m	2.76m	11.5t	220hp	28+67
MAN NG274	18.00m	2.50m	2.76m	?	?	?
Mercedes Citaro	11.95m	2.55m	3.08m	11.5t	279hp	38+55
Citélis	11.99m	2.50m	2.93m	10.38t	245hp	31+64
Gruau microbus	5.38m	1.99m	2.95m	2.33t	?	9+13

Fleet numbering

Brillié-Schneider PB double-deckers	1-150
Schneider P3	1-97
Schneider PB2	201-718, 801-909
De Dion OA	1001-1263
Schneider H	1-1269
Schneider H6	5001-5051
Renault KX1	6016-6030
Somua	6001-6015
Renault PN	1301-1637
Renault PY	6031-6053
Renault TN4 A1	6054-6203
Renault TN4 A2	1638-1957
Renault TN 6A	1958-2727
Renault TN6 C1	6204-6293
Renault TN6 C2	2728-2887
Renault TN4 C	2938-2987
Panhard K63 A	2888-2937
Panhard K63 B	3273-3337
Renault TN4 F	2988-3272
Renault ZYAE	6294-6303
Panhard ZUROC	6304-6313
Panhard K63 CP	3598-3657
Panhard K63 CB	3918-3977
Panhard K63 D	4428-4527
Renault TN4 HP	3338-3597, 3978-4127
Renault TN4 H BAR	4258-4277, 4298-4427
Renault TN4 H BAL	3658-3828, 3892-3917, 4128-4257

(Some Renault TN4F/TN4H that are retained for private hire have been renumbered 901-9.)

Prototype 6001	Built in workshops
Prototype 6002	Somua OP 5
Prototype 6003	SNCASO
Chausson APH47 & 48	1-56
Chausson VBRH	8051-8100
Somua OP 5 2	501-801
Renault R4200	301-326
Chausson AHH521	125-128, 285/6
Chausson APH50 and 52	55-124, 275-284
Chausson APU	1001-1273
Somua OP 5 3	321-500 and 802-1000
Berliet PCP 10	1401-1500
Chausson APU	130-227, 1275-1400 and 1741-2212
VBF	8106-8143
Somua OP 5 3 SB 3	1501-1740
Berliet PCS10	1-5
Saviem prototype Standard	4450
Berliet prootype Standard	4451
Verney prototype Standard	4452
Verney RU	4501-4560
Standard SC10	5101-7475, 7486-7855, 7901-9350
Berliet PCM-R	4151-4500 and 4601-5000
Berliet PCM-RE double-deck	2200-2225
Berliet PGR	2441-3000
Berliet PR100 PA	4001-4010
Berliet PR100MI	4011-30
Renault PR100MI	4031-107

Renault PR100.2	4108-204
Saviem E	5001-5010
Saviem SC10 (open platform)	7476-7485 and 7856-7900
Saviem SC10R	9351-9999 and 3001-3947
Heuliez	4301/2
Renault minibuses	11-38
Citroën HWCH14/Currus minibuses	101-118
Saviem SB2 minibuses	119-124
Citroën C35/Heuliez minibuses	201-17
CBM220-Heuliez midibuses	601-618
Peugeot J9/Durisotti	301/2
Mercedes O305	501 experimental bus 1976-7
Scania BR111M/Jonckheere	502 experimental bus 1976-7
Volvo B59-55/Jonckheere	503 experimental bus 1976-7
Magirus-Deutz	504 experimental bus 1976-7
Renault PR180	4501-4937
Saviem SC10R	3948-3981 (open platform)
Renault R312	5001, 5003 and 5011-6604
Renault R212	500/1 ex-Auto Nice Transport
Heuliez GX77 midibuses	651-668
Heuliez GX317	1001-1124
Heuliez GX317	8001-8057 (LPG)
Van Hool A500	505 experimental bus 1990-92
Kässbohrer S300NC	506 experimental bus 1990-92
Mercedes O405N	507 experimental bus 1990-92
Renault Agora	2001-2576, 2578-2892, 2577 prototype gas bus, not taken into stock
Renault Agora	7201-7953
Renault Agora GNV	7001-7053 (7039 was burned out before entering service and replaced by a new vehicle with the same number)
Renault Agora L (articulated)	1501-1650, 1701-1809 and 4401-4571
Peugeot J9/Durisotti minibuses	301/2 (nos. later reused)
Mercedes-Benz OA412 minibuses	801-849, 851/2 and 861-865
Mercedes-Benz Citaro	4251-4320
Heuliez GX117 midibuses	401-412, 415-433, 451-460
Gruau MG36 battery minibuses	301/2 (1996 reused numbers)
Ponticelli TU35/Amiot	401
Ponticelli MG36/Gruau	411-414
Oréos 55 midibuses	303-314 since renumbered 1303-1314
Irisbus Agora	8101-8520
Scania Omnicity articulated	1681-1691
Scania S	9301-9376, still being delivered
A508 MAN/Van Hool midibuses	711-718
Gruau microbuses	720-739
MAN NL223	9001-9205
MAN NG274	4601-4615
Irisbus Citélis	3001-3366 still being delivered

Other private hire vehicles are:

Renault Master	911-4	(2001)
Renault/Carrier	920	(secondhand)
MAN 469NIC/ACEV	921-3	(2001)
??/Carrier	925	(c2006)

Organisation of Paris Buses

Unlike that of London, the bus network in Paris has always been divided into city and suburban sections, the latter more recently having been further divided into inner- and outer-suburban sections. As will be seen from the fleet history, this division has had a considerably effect on vehicle design.

The network within Paris comprises lines linking one of the former city gates (Porte de...), or a nearby point, with a terminus in the centre. In 1964 these lines had an average length of 9.3km, (5.8 miles) and therefore much shorter than urban services in London and Berlin. The RATP and its predecessors have not at any time favoured long lines such as are found in these cities, considering that these would be difficult to run efficiently. An exception to this rule are the lines which form the Petite Ceinture (PC), a service which, until December 2006, had a total length of 34km. As already mentioned, however, it had latterly to be divided into three services, as traffic congestion had made it impossible to maintain regularity over so great a distance. On 16 December 2006 the bus service on the southern part of the ring was replaced by tram line T3 and further sections will be similarly converted within the next few years.

The urban network to-day consists of 55 lines, numbered variously between 20 and 96, plus the three services making up the PC network, numbered PC1, 2 and 3. Of the 55 lines, 17 are or will be classified as "Mobilien" and 38 are ordinary services. There is also the Montmartrobus" (Pigalle – Mairie du 18e.) and a tourist line "Balabus", which runs from Gare de Lyon to La Défense between April and September only. The latter is worked by normal service buses, not in any special livery. In addition, as mentioned above, there are various lines worked by midi- or minibuses.

Since line numbers replaced the former letter system on urban lines after the second world war, the numbering scheme has been based on the following principles. The first digit indicates the city terminus, as follows : 2, Gare Saint-Lazare, 3, Gare de l'Est, 4, Gare du Nord, 5 and 6, other termini on the Right Bank of the Seine, 7, Hôtel de Ville, 8, other termini on the Left Bank and 9, Gare Montparnasse. The second digit indicates the area of the outer terminus, as follows : 2, south-west of the city, 3 and 4, north-west, 5, north and north-east, 6, east and south-east, 7 and 8 and 9, south. The scheme is extremely logical, but over the years a few exceptions have had to be made to it as traffic flows change. However, most numbers are still in accordance with the outline given above and a knowledge of the numbering system can be of great help to the visitor to the city. Thus line 27 is Gare Saint-Lazare – Porte de Vitry, while line 38 is Gare du Nord – Porte d'Orléans (unusually, the latter runs parallel to a Métro line (4) for much of its length) and line 80 is Mairie du 18e – Porte de Versailles. The evening service (service en soirée) runs from about 20.30 to 00.30 on 16 lines only, plus the three PC lines, and a reduced service is operated Sundays and public holidays on 28 lines, again plus the PC lines. About 20 city lines do penetrate the suburbs, such as line 39, from Gare de l'Est to Issy – Val de Seine, but only in the case of line 24 (to Maison Alfort) is the distance beyond the city boundary very long.

At 13.9km, line 24 is in fact the longest urban line, apart from the Balabus. Apart from Montmartrobus, the shortest line is the 63 (Opéra – Clichy, Victor Hugo). Leaving aside the PC services, each of which until 2006 carried over 16 million passengers per year, the three busiest lines are 62, 55 and 27, each of which carries over 11 million passengers per year.

The suburban network is made up mainly of lines which fan outwards from terminal stations of the Metro, together with some peripheral lines linking suburban communities and also serving suburban railway stations. In 2007 there was a total of 191 lines operated by RATP, together with 49 lines which were operated under contract by private companies. These figures represent a route length of 2,122km. Through the Association Professionelle des Transports Routiers (APTR), private operators are responsible for 11 other lines and 33 lines are worked on behalf of the Département de Seine-Saint Denis. Suburban lines are generally fairly short, having in 1964 an average length of only 8km (5 miles), but by 2007 this had risen to 10.9km. They generally have a higher average speed than those in the central area. Apart from the fact that line numbers run from 100 upwards, there is no particular numbering scheme for suburban services, numbers having been used as services have developed. Since the 1950s outer suburban services have also been developed, to serve the growing communities of what is poetically called "Le banlieue de la Grande Couronne", which can be translated into English only as the prosaic "outer suburban area". These services are generally based on railway stations and maintain a high average speed, of the order of 21km/hr in 1964. They were the first to be operated by on a one-man basis (it was invariably a man in those days) and in the 1950s and '60s were entirely worked by Chausson buses. Many inner suburban lines share their inner terminus with urban services, at places such as Porte d'Orléans, where ten suburban services have their inner terminus. The busiest suburban line is 183 (Porte de Choisy – Aéroport d'Orly), with over 16 million annual passengers. It must also be the straightest line in Paris, since it runs in a direct line from its inner terminus for 8km to Les Saules and has only two right-angled turns thereafter! Because of its heavy traffic, there has been consideration of converting this service to a tram line. As in the city area, there is a reduced evening service in the suburban area from 20.30 to 00.30, but there is no special network on Sundays and holidays.

The RATP had served Orly airport from its opening in 1961 with line 285 from Place d'Italie and there were also local services to the former airport at Le Bourget, which was replaced by Roissy – later Roissy-Charles de Gaulle. However, none of these particularly attracted air travellers and in 1983 it was decided to institute special airport services. That to Orly, known as Orlybus, starts from

LEFT: Many of the Mercedes-Benz Citaro vehicles are used on stopping services to the airports. 4278 is seen at the inner terminus of line 351 to Roissy, at Nation – Place des Antilles, on 16 April 2008. *(Author)*

Denfert-Rochereau station on RER line B, while Roissybus starts from Opéra. They have proved popular with air travellers and those who work at the airports and both are now worked by articulated vehicles. In 2003 Orlybus carried two million passengers and Roissybus 1.4 million. The airports are of course also served by local lines.

Night services were at one time, as in London, very poor, but this has changed in recent years and today the network known as *Noctilien* (night people) provides extensive coverage of the entire Ile-de-France Region, running from the time when rail services close down around 00.30 until they resume next morning at 05.30. This system was introduced in September 2005, in conjunction with SNCF. There are 35 lines, all prefixed with the letter N. Within Paris, these are organised around five interchange points, at St-Lazaare, Montparnasse, Gare de l'Est, Gare du Nord and Châtelet and two circular services, N01 and N02, link all but the last of these, as well as serving many popular night spots. These two lines run every 17 minutes from Sunday to Thursday and every ten minutes at week-ends. Lines N11 to N16 inclusive are urban services, generally following Métro lines and running every half hour during the week and every 10 to 15 minutes at week-ends. Thus line N16, from Pont de Levallois to Mairie de Montreuil, basically runs along the route of Métro line 3. From several of the main line railway stations, 19 lines fan out to serve outer suburban areas beyond the city and to a large extent cover the RER network. Line N32, for example, runs from Gare de Lyon to Boissy-Saint-Léger, basically the eastern section of RER line A. These lines are numbered between N21 and N63; they run at least every hour, but may have a 20 min frequency on certain sections. Finally eight lines, numbered N121 to N151, run from Paris to outer suburbs, again basically along the routes of RER or main line suburban services. These are worked by coaches, rather than by service buses, and have an hourly or half-hourly frequency. Both airports are linked to the city by the Noctilien network.

The Noctilien services have proved very popular and have made it much easier for Parisians and visitors to enjoy a night out without having to forego the pleasure of a glass or two with a meal!

Depots

Scarcely anything is known about the depots used by the various companies before 1855. Only by a process of deduction has it been possible to ascertain the location of some of these. That of Vaugirard, for example, was used by Les Favorites, while it is likely that the depots of Barrière-Blanche, Bastille, and Saint-Mandé belonged to the Entreprise Générale. On its formation, the CGO had to set about acquiring a number of new sites suitable for building the kind of depots it envisaged and it immediately opened at least four, and possibly five, new depots in 1855. When it began operations, it had 25 depots in the city and nine in the suburbs, housing 4,300 horses. Most of those taken over from the smaller companies were leased, but the CGO preferred to own its properties and for all its new depots bought the sites outright. By 1867 it had 44 depots, of which it owned 26 and leased 18.

Due to the size of its fleet and the number of horses it required, the CGO had a large number of depots. It was clearly not possible to locate all of these in suburban areas, as many had to be adjacent to the termini of lines within the city, to allow for easy exchange of horses, and the company therefore had to buy sites in prime areas, although it seems to have managed to do so for reasonable amounts. The CGO had to pay the 'octroi' – a tax levied on goods being brought into the pre-1860 area of the city, on all fodder being brought in to those depots and this considerably inflated its costs. The city authorities, however, insisted in 1879 that all depots had to be in its area, unless a special tax was paid and all but three depots were therefore located within the pre-1860 boundaries. One of the largest, for example, was situated in Boulevard Bourdon, at Bastille. The average area of one depot in 1867 was 3,155 square metres, most of which was occupied by the stables and the other facilities necessary to feed and care for the stud of horses. The area actually occupied by the vehicles was relatively small. To minimise expenditure, the CGO developed the concept of a depot with stables on an upper level, reached by a gently-sloping ramp. Saint-Martin, opened about 1866, was the first depot of this layout. Harnesses were hung from the ceiling on the ground floor and a farrier's shop was incorporated in the complex, as horses had to be shod regularly to give their hooves a good grip on the wood block paving generally used on Paris streets at the time. Storage of fodder was in the basement and new supplies were brought in by wagon and sent down chutes to these stores. The fodder was then made up into bags containing a mixture of the various kinds used and hoisted up to the level of the stables, where the grain went through a mincer to break it into small pieces. There was also an infirmary for sick horses and this was visited daily by a vet. For staff there was a surgery, visited by a doctor on a rotational basis ; those who had been diagnosed as unwell were then treated by the doctor at home. Very often housing for the depot staff and crews was also incorporated in the complex.

The '*chef*', assisted by one or two '*piqueurs*' (head stablemen), was the head of the depot and was responsible not only for its staff and horses, but also for the bus crews and the 'cochers' who had charge of trace horses. A large number of men were required to run each depot and the labour force consisted of grooms (*palefreniers*), wheelwrights (*charrons*), washers (*laveurs*), farriers (*marechaux-ferrants*) and lamp men (*lampistes*). The '*chef*' had to send a daily report to head office on the staff, the horses and the stores of fodder and at the end of each turn of duty, conductors had to submit to him their waybill and takings. Managing an establishment of this kind must have called for considerable administrative skills, in addition to an ability to handle men and horses.

The origins of Clichy depot went back to at least 1842, when two of the smaller private operators – Les Batignollaises and Les Gazelles – merged and opened a joint depot on the site, in Avenue de Clichy. The CGO took this over in 1855 and renamed it Batignolles-Clichy, but it did not actually own the buildings until 1864. It was rebuilt in 1906 and was the first depot to operate motor buses. Taking advantage of the rebuilding, the roof was made high enough to accommodate the Brillié-Schneider P2 class and much later, because of its headroom, Clichy also operated the Berliet double-deckers of 1968. It closed in October 1989. When trams were introduced in the 1870s, two bus depots, Alma and Monge, were adapted to house both buses and trams.

CGO bus depots in 1899

Allemagne (Alexandre Dumas), Alma (T), Bagnolet, Batignolles-Clichy, Belleville, Bîcetre, Billancourt, Bourdon, Charenton, Contrescarpe, Courbevoie, Curial, Gare d'Ivry, Gobelins, Grenelle I and II, Haxo, Jemappes, Lebrun, Maine, Malesherbes, Monceaux, Monge (T), Montmartre, Montreuil, Panthéon, Plaisance, Puebla, Pyrénées, Ternes, La Vallée, Vaugirard, La Villette, Vincennes.

T: also housed trams

An immediate result of the conversion to motor vehicles was a considerable reduction in the number of depots. No longer was it necessary to have a depot close to virtually every line and no longer did the CGO have to use expensive sites in the city centre, since motor buses could easily run some distance to and from a depot when entering or coming out of service. Depots were now also relatively smaller in the total surface area per vehicle. The CGO was able to reduce the number of bus depots from the 34 listed above to eleven. The new depot of Lebrun, for example, opened in 1912, with a surface area of 7,750 square metres, while the much larger depot of Croix-Nivert (1910) replaced three former depots and housed both buses and trams. A central distribution point for petrol was constructed at Saint-Ouen, in the north of the city.

On its formation, the STCRP inherited 23 depots from the former tramway companies, in addition to those of the CGO mentioned above, and in the 1920s instituted a policy of rationalisation. Some depots were closed, others modernised and/or enlarged and others became simply sub-depots of larger ex-CGO depots. These measures did not greatly affect the bus system, but in the course of the modernisation programme, eight establishments became combined bus and tram depots. With the tramway conversion scheme of the 1930s, no fewer than 18 tram depots were converted to take buses and the former joint depots became buses only. On the outbreak of war in 1939, the STCRP possessed 27 depots. Poissoniers was destroyed in 1946 and its area added to that of the central workshops. Mozart was converted to house the driving school and Bastille became the base for the breakdown fleet, for both road services and the Métro. Other depots were closed for a time or used to house stored vehicles and by 1964 the number of active depots had been reduced to 20, plus two sub-depots.

Depots in 1964

North-west

Asnières	90 (T)	
Charlebourg	200 (T)	
Clichy	90	
Gonesse	150 (T). Closed in 1966, replaced by a new building.	
Malesherbes	70	
Michelet	88 (T) Closed 1970, used since then for RATP vans and lorries	
Port-Marly	15 (sub-depot)	
Puteaux	70 (T) Closed in 1976	

East

Flandre	200 (T)
Hainaut	130 (T) Closed 1991
Lagny	150 (T)
La Maltournée	200 (T)
Le Raincy	50 (T) (sub-depot)
Les Lilas	240 (T)
Saint-Mandé	? (T) Closed 1971, became transport museum from 1973 to 1998
Saint-Maur	100 (T)

South

Croix-Nivert	145 (T)
Ivry	250 (including trolleybuses)
Lebrun	84
Malakoff	145 (T)
Montrouge	200 (T).
Point-du-Jour	165 (T)

(T) former tram depot

As the geographical location of these did not always correspond with current requirements, the RATP in 1959 drew up a programme for the renewal of its installations. Seven depots would be maintained as they were, five would be enlarged to take 200 vehicles, ten depots of a similar capacity would be built in the suburbs and nine small depots would be closed. Lack of finance prevented the full implementation of this programme, but several, such as Les Lilas, were enlarged. This work was carried out while normal services were still operating, no easy task for either depot staff or crews. Four were opened between 1969 and 1976 and two large new depots – Belliard and Aubervilliers – were built to replace Clichy and Hainault and opened between 1987 and 1999. Four smaller depots were closed. The introduction of the Standard design led to simplification of maintenance and overhauls were now based on a timetable, instead of the number of kilometres run.

Depots in 2008

These are now known as 'Centres Bus' and sub-depots are 'Relais Bus'.

Asnières
First opened in 1876 or 1877 to house the trams of the Tramways Nord. It passed to the TPDS in 1881. It housed steam trams from 1891 and electric trams from 1897. It closed after service on 14 April 1936 and re-opened as a bus garage on 21 December of the same year. Present capacity 103 vehicles.

Aubervilliers
Opened in 1997. Capacity 216.

Belliard
Opened in 1987. Capacity 196.

Bord de Marne – Neuilly
Opened after 1980. Capacity 186

Charlebourg
Built by the STCRP as a tram depot in 1925. Closed to trams on New Year's Eve 1934 and re-opened for buses on 5 August 1935. Present capacity 184.

Créteil
Opened in 1971. Capacity 167

Croix-Nivert
Built by the CGO in 1911 as a bus and tram depot. It ceased to house trams in June 1930 and was closed during the second world war. Re-opened in 1951, it now has a capacity of 115 vehicles.

Flandre (Pantin)
Built as a horse tram depot for the Tramways Nord in 1876/7 and modified for electric trams in 1899. Buses were first housed in this depot in June 1934 and the last tram left on 21 December 1936. Capacity is 185.

Fontenay-aux-roses
Opened in 1969. Capacity 218.

Lagny
Ex-tram depot, built by the CGO in 1877. Closed to trams on 5 December 1932. Present capacity 110.

Les Lilas
Opened in 1900 as a tram depot for the Est Parisien Company and at that time the largest depot in the Paris area. Buses first used it on 17 December 1934 and it closed to trams on 11 February 1935. Present capacity 213. This depot also houses the double-deck buses used on L'Open Tour.

Malakoff
Built as a tram depot by the Tramways Sud in 1876 and enlarged by the CGPT in 1901. Became a bus depot on 15 March 1937. Present capacity 200. From 1957 to 1973 part of the 1901 extension housed the AMTUIR museum.

Montrouge
Built by the CGO as a tram depot in 1883 and became a bus garage on 3 March 1937. Capacity 127

Nanterre
Opened in 1976. Capacity 223.

Pavillons-sous-Bois
Opened in 1972. Capacity 185.

Pleyel
Opened in 1969 Capacity 197.

Point de Jour
Built as a tram depot by the CGO in 1857. Housed compressed air trams from 1894 and electric trams from 1906. Modernised in 1911/1912. Became a bus garage on 2 September 1935. Capacity 120.

Quai de Seine Ivry
Built as a tram depot by the CGPT in 1907. Became a bus garage on 14 April 1934. Capacity 152.

Saint-Denis (Also known as Gonesse)
Opened in 1965. Capacity 212.

Thiais
Opened in 1969. Capacity 169.

Vitry
Capacity 189

There are also four sub-depots, Bord de Marne Bussy (75 buses), Montrouge Massy (74), Créteil (Saint-Maur) (93) and Quai de Seine (Lebrun) (67). Créteil is an ex-tram depot.

Aubervilliers also houses the driver training school.

Capacity figures may vary where articulated vehicles are involved.

TOP: An exterior view of Montrouge depot in September 2008. *(Author)*

ABOVE: The interior of the same depot, with Agora 2823 about to leave to take up service on line 188. *(Author)*

ABOVE RIGHT: MAN 9002 has been receiving some attention in the maintenance area of Montrouge on 20th September 2008. *(Author)*

RIGHT: A large fleet of auxiliary vehicles is maintained to keep services running smoothly. This mobile crane is at Montrouge on the same day. *(Author)*

Maintenance Programmes and the Central Workshops

When it was formed in 1855, the CGO inherited from the Entreprise des Omnibus a large workshop at 50 Rue des Poissoniers in the northern suburb of La Chapelle, at that date actually outwith the city area. In this workshop the CGO built a fleet of 828 double-deck horse buses between 1855 and 1860. With the extension of the city's boundaries in 1860, the workshops were now within its area and were considerably extended. Despite this, they were by 1878 no longer adequate and in 1880 more land was acquired in the rue Championnet, between the rue de Mont-Cenis and the rue des Poissoniers. On this land the CGO used the metal framework from one of the pavilions of the 1878 Exposition to build a large new workshop. The new complex, known as l'Atelier Central (Central Workshop) was opened in 1883 and the old buildings were subsequently sold and demolished. It catered not only for the fleet of horse buses but also of horse trams and, subsequently, for the weird and wonderful variety of mechanically-powered trams used by the CGO from the 1890s onwards. From 1906 it also maintained motor buses and, after the creation of the STCRP, became also the main tramway workshops for the entire Paris network. Over the years, many bodies for both buses and trams were also constructed. From 1938 only buses were maintained.

During the second world war, the workshop staff had the unenviable task of trying to keep the fleet on the road and also that of modifying buses to run on other fuels. However, part of the complex and labour force were used by the occupying forces to manufacture parts for weapons, this work being generally carried out as slowly and inefficiently as possible and occasionally hindered by sabotage by members of the Resistance among the staff. The eastern part of the works was badly damaged by bombing on 21st April 1944, fortunately without any injury to personnel, and had to be extensively rebuilt ; not until that task was completed was it possible to catch up with the arrears of maintenance of the war years.

The introduction of the Standard, with its ease of maintenance and the reduction in vehicle life to a maximum of twelve years greatly diminished the volume of work being undertaken by the workshops. It also led to the cessation of bodybuilding there. There was therefore a significant revision in organisation and methods within the workshops, with a consequent reduction in staff. As a result the workshops were once again considered to be out of date and in the 1980s underwent another substantial rebuilding, which sadly involved the demolition of the 1878 buildings.

Traffic

There has in recent years been a gratifying increase in the number of passengers using surface transport. In 2005 the bus and tram network carried 991.3 million passengers, this figure being divided between 335.1m on bus lines in Paris, 594.6m on suburban lines and 61.6m on the trams and the Val de Marne Busway. This represented 2,763.9m passenger/km with an average journey length of 2.79km. Average speed was 13km/hr within Paris and 17.7km/hr in the suburbs, this latter figure being somewhat inflated by the inclusion of the trams and the lines using the Busway. Just ten years before, the total number of passengers carried was just under 800m, while in 1975 it was only 570.2m.

Passengers carried

	Passengers, in millions	Vehicle-kilometres run
1930	943.3	175
1938	748.4	171.4
1946	602.9	69.8
1948	898.2	105.9
1958	873.7	124
1968	543.3	172
1978	709.2	131.9
1995	795	Not known
2006	924.6*	138.7*

*This does not include figures for the Val-de-Marne busway, as these are included with the tramway totals.

Fares and Tickets

In the days of horse buses, no tickets were actually issued when a passenger paid a single fare. The conductor registered the transaction by pulling on a bell rope, which recorded it on a register. He also made a mark on his waybill. This contained details of the number of passengers carried, per journey, inside and on the upper deck being shown separately. Passengers joining with a transfer were also shown separately. Waybills were checked several times on each trip by "controleurs" (inspectors) at stations. An example which has been preserved is a waybill for the line Madeleine-Bastille for 6 July 1866. This shows that the bus made 20 trips, the average duration of which was 30 minutes. In the course of the day, 474 passengers were carried and 105.45 francs taken in receipts. In 1870 fares were 30 centimes for travel inside, with free transfer, and 15 centimes for travel on top, with a transfer costing an additional 15c. These figures would have been roughly equivalent to 6d and 3d in sterling at the time. Employees enjoyed free travel when of duty and were given a "ticket franchise" to confirm their status, while military personnel also travelled free and were given an exchange ticket in return for their service. Conductors must have found the paper work quite a burden, but the general level of honesty seems to have been high and little money found its way into individual pockets. To put these fares into perspective, it should be mentioned that the price of the daily newspaper "Le Figaro" in 1900 was 15 centimes. Members of the upper classes used the buses quite often and ladies travelling on their own could do so with perfect security.

Despite the number of companies running buses before 1855, a system of "correspondance" (transfer) was instituted in 1840, when there were 160 points at which it was possible to transfer between buses of both the same and another company. It is not clear how the various companies arranged the finances of this scheme between them. While no tickets were issued to passengers making a single trip, it was obviously necessary to have some kind of check for the system of "correspondances". Originally this was done by issuing flimsy paper tickets torn from a roll, but in 1863 there were replaced by card tickets, similar to those used on main line railways. When using these, passengers had to show the ticket to the "controleur" at the designated transfer station and receive in exchange a queue ticket for the connecting bus. The ticket was no longer valid if a passenger went away from the station while waiting and was not there when the number was called. This limited fraudulent use of such tickets. Tickets were printed in various colours, but buff with a vertical green band seems to have been common, and they were overprinted with symbols such as a Saint Andrew's cross, again in the interest of prevention of misuse. Tickets were also overprinted with the line's code letter. All tickets also showed "intérieur" or "impériale" for travel inside or on top respectively and in the latter case, they were also marked with three red diagonal lines.

153 PARIS - La Bourse
The Change House

RIGHT: Until 1939 many services terminated at the Bourse (Stock Exchange); this post card view was taken about 1912. Although begun in 1808 under Napoléon I, the building was not finished until 1828. On the left a De Dion Bouton approaches the bus station, while on the right a line of taxis waits at the kerb. *(Author's collection)*

This system lasted more or less without change or increase in fares until 1910 and there was no mechanisation of ticket issue comparable to the use of the Bell punch machine in Britain. However, when the new concessions came into force, all passengers were, from 1st June of that year, required to have a ticket and each line was now divided into several sections. As 1st and 2nd class had now replaced the former distinction between inside and upper deck, a very wide variety of coloured paper tickets came into use to cope with all possible variations and it is impossible to list them all in this summary. Tickets for one section, which cost 10 centimes, were geographical and gave the names of the first and last stops within that section. Tickets for more than one section did not carry any place names. It was also possible to upgrade from second to first class on payment of a supplement of 5 cents and a ticket was issued to cover this. Fares in first class were 15c, 25c and 50c, while in second they were 10c and 15c. Tickets for one section were common to both buses and trams, but for more than one section, in first class, different tickets were used, since fares differed, and these were designated "tramway" or "omnibus". Correspondance tickets were no longer issued.

The new system seems to have worked quite well initially, but was soon interrupted by the outbreak of war and the cessation of all services. The inflation of the immediate post-war years brought several fare increases and, as stocks of the old tickets remained, these were adapted by use of a perforation to show the new fares. As small change was scarce at this time, metal tokens, known as "tickets métalliques" were issued in denominations of 20, 25 and 30 centimes, between 1921 and 1923.

On 19 January 1922 an agreement was signed between the STCRP and the Département, maintaining the basic principles of section fares, the two-class system and instituting a different scale of fares for suburban journeys. All bus and tram fares were harmonised and fares were increased. In second class these were now 25c for one section within Paris and 40c for two sections, with fares of additional 10c for each further section. In the suburbs, fares were based on distance, being charged at 8c per km in second class. Workmen's tickets were also made available on the bus network, giving a return journey for at single fare before 07.00 in the suburbs and 08.00 within Paris. Military personnel disabled in the recent war were also given a special tariff.

As traffic grew, the manual system of ticket issue, involving a cash transaction for every fare, became more and more difficult to work efficiently and fraud also increased. It was recognised that ticket issue would have to be mechanised and the first trials of a Klein-Massot ticket cancelling machine took place late in 1927. These were successful and the system was extended to the entire network by 1932. The issue of "carnets" (books) of 20 tickets had also been instituted on 5 December 1927. At price of FR5, these offered a considerable discount on cash fares, which now became 30cm per section in second class, and most passengers took advantage of this. The "carnets" were issued in covers tastefully illustrated with views of famous buildings, such as the Paris Opera, or famous Frenchmen, Jules Verne being thus honoured. Famous Frenchwomen seem to have been overlooked! They also carried advertising material for both STCRP services and commercial products. The tickets now came in concertina strips of ten and a passenger simply detached the required number and presented them to the conductor for cancellation. The machine used for this was fairly light and cancellation was effected by turning a handle on the left hand side. Officially this was known as an "appareil oblitérateur enregistreur" (cancellation and recording machine), but to passengers and crews alike it was a "moulinette" (little mill) or "moulin à café" (coffee mill). Workmen's weekly tickets, were also introduced at this time. These were valid for six days and could be issued for any line in the network, but were specific to that line. In 1930, weekly tickets valid for a given number of sections and valid for either five or six days anywhere on the STCRP network were introduced. All sections were now fixed at 2.5km and within Paris the maximum number of sections charged was limited to three.

The STCRP had greatly eased the work of the conductors with these changes and the new system was adopted by them with enthusiasm. The machines of this type remained in use until 1965. It was all much in advance of current practice in London, where the Bell Punch still reigned supreme and where every passenger had to pay in cash for every fare.

As mentioned above, there were fare increases in the late 1930s, but the system was not altered in any way until the take-over of the STCRP by the CMP in 1941. The new administration harmonised all fares, based on the creation of a module U, equivalent to the charge for one section on a bus line and fixed at the 1939 fare of 65 centimes. However, as the length of one section was now reduced to 1.25km, this represented a considerable increase The Metro ticket now cost 2U in second class and 3U in first. As some bus lines in the suburbs comprised ten sections, a maximum fare of 6U was fixed for all bus services. First class fares on the bus network were abolished at the same time. The weekly tickets were then withdrawn, but soon reappeared in a slightly different form, being available for combined Métro+bus journeys between a suburb and central Paris. To take account of the occupation, a special, bilingual ticket at FR2 was issued for the use of German military personnel travelling in

uniform. Propaganda appeared on the covers of the carnets. As cardboard was, like everything else in occupied France, in very short supply, tickets valid for two journeys and sold in carnets of five, were issued from 21 March 1943 and did not disappear until 1 August 1958. However, the alignment of bus and Métro fares did not cause any change in the methods of fare collection, though in due course the initials STCRP disappeared and were replaced by a simple M. In 1949 this was in turn replaced by the initials RATP. When peace returned in 1945, the section length was increased to 1.5km. in 1947 a half-fare ticket for "famille nombreuse" (large family) came into operation. Fares were increased frequently in this period and from 1945, when U=FR1, it had risen to FF5 by October 1948.

It was the change to driver-only operation, when drivers became "agents receveurs" (driver conductors) which finally brought to an end the carnet of concertina tickets and the ticket cancelling machines. They were replaced by new single tickets sold by drivers, to be cancelled in the new on-board machines. In October 1968 a new and slightly longer style of card ticket was issued, this being available either on the Métro (and very soon also on the RER within Paris) or on the bus network, on which it was valid for two sections. This was coloured ivory and carried the wording "Métro ou autobus". From September 1973, all tickets had a longitudinal magnetic strip along the back. They were now coloured bright yellow and in due course this ticket became the focus of a very successful advertising campaign, with the slogan "ticket chic, ticket choc".

A much more radical change was brought about by the introduction of the Carte Orange on 1st July 1975. There were three main aims in the creation of the new system – to remove the penalty involved when a passenger changed from one mode of transport to another, to make long journeys relatively less expensive and to bring in what was effectively a multi-modal season ticket. The new system was put into effect by the creation of five concentric zones, working outwards from the centre of Paris. A photocard was issued and passengers used this in conjunction with an orange monthly coupon for the number of zones in which they wished to travel. The Carte was valid on all forms of transport within the area (including bus lines in the suburbs worked by operators other than RATP) and was brought into use on 1st July 1975. In 1982 a weekly coupon, coloured yellow, became available, as did an annual ticket, the latter being renamed Carte Intégrale on 1st May 1984. Passengers did not cancel the coupons on boarding a bus and this operation was thus speeded up. The new one-day version of the Carte Orange was known as Formule 1 but, unlike the Carte Orange was not valid on APTR buses. It was renamed Mobilis in April 1997 and extended to Zone 8 and APTR/ADATRIF buses. On New Year's Day 1991 the area of the Carte Orange was extended to cover the entire Région of Ile-de-France and it was of course extended to the trams when they came into service in July 1992. The success of the new system was immediate and, as detailed elsewhere, it had a very considerable effect on the number of passengers using the bus network. By 1976 it was estimated that 40% of all RATP passengers used the Carte Orange, while in 2006 there were (excluding students) 3.2 million holders of some form of weekly, monthly and annual ticket and the total purchased numbered 43.5 million, to which should be added 8 million short term tickets such as Mobilis. The new system did not bring to an end the use of ordinary tickets, which were and are still available, either singly or in carnets of ten, and are cancelled on boarding a bus or tram as before, but 60% of all passengers in Ile-de-France now travel on some kind of card. When the RATP introduced its new corporate design, in March 1992, the ordinary ticket became jade green, this changing to mauve in 2003. Special tickets are issued for the airport services of Roissybus and Orlybus.

The next major change to the fare system happened very recently. On 1 July 2007 the Ticket+ was introduced, reviving the "correspondance" of early years. This ticket is valid for 1hr30mins from the time of cancellation and allows multiple transfer from one bus line to another, or from bus to tram, during this period. It can be used on Noctilien services, but without the transfer facility. It is not valid on airport services and on a few very long bus lines – over 12.5km in length – a second ticket has to be cancelled. It is of course also valid on the Métro, with transfer between lines as before, and on the RER within Paris. Origin-destination tickets for rail journeys were also introduced and these can also be bought as a carnet. They are not valid on buses, trams on lines T1 and T3 or the Montmartre funicular. At the same time the two outermost zones were merged into Zone 6, bringing about a considerable reduction in fares for long-distance commuters using a Carte Orange. The Ticket+ can be bought in a carnet of ten, with a considerable saving over individual tickets.

Special tickets for visitors from abroad were first issued in March 1953. These were valid for seven days and a four-day version appeared in 1970, when these tickets were also made available to French visitors from outwith Paris. A two-day ticket was sold from May 1979. In may 1982 the ticket was renamed "Paris Sésaame" and came with a magnetic coupon, similar to that of the Carte Orange. In June 1989 it was possible to use it also on suburban trains of SNCF and it then became "Paris Visite". For visitors, the tickets most likely to be useful are Mobilis and Paris

Visite. The former is a day ticket, issued in five combinations of zones from 1-2 to 1-6. It cannot be used on airport services, although it is valid on normal lines serving airports, such as line 183 at Orly. It is personal and the holder must write her/his name on it, with the date, before first cancelling it. It must be validated each time the holder boards a bus or tram. Paris Visite is available for one, two, three or five consecutive days and allows travel on airport services. It comes in two combinations of zone – 1-3 or 1-6. Special tickets are also from time to time issued to commemorate developments such as the opening of an extension to the Métro or its centenary in 2000, important sporting events and cultural happenings, such as European gay pride in 1997, for which a pink ticket was issued, a colour new to the RATP.

Tariffs in 2008 were as follows:- (All prices in Euros)

Ticket+, single ticket	1.50
Carnet of ten tickets	11.10
Orlybus	6.10
Roissybus	8.10
RER Paris-Charles de Gaulle	8.60
RER Paris-Rungis-orly	6.00

Cartre Orange coupons are available for zones 1-2, 1-3, 1-4, 1-5, 1-6 and 2-3, 2-4 and 2-5. They are issued in weekly and monthly versions and the former is valid only from Monday to Sunday. The monthly ticket is valid for one calendar month. A photocard is necessary. From May 2008 the Carte Orange will be valid only with a pass Navigo, which must be bought in advance and eight days should be allowed for processing a first request for this pass. As an example of fares using a Carte Orange, zones 1-2 cost EUR16.30 for one week or 53.50 for one month.

Passengers should retain tickets as long as they are on board a bus or tram or until they leave a station at the end of a journey. Exits are clearly marked "Limite de validité des billets". Ticket checks are fairly frequent and are often carried out by plain clothes officers, both on board or in passageways in stations. Visitors should take care NOT to buy tickets from people who offer them for sale, very often in main line stations. These are tickets which have been picked up from the ground and their validity will have expired. Anyone caught using one could face a heavy fine.

There are of course reduced tickets for children and young people and for special groups, such as people with mobility difficulties.

ROW 1: the top two are typical of the correspondance [transfer] tickets issued on Edmondson-type cards from 1863 till probably 1910 – believed to be bus or tram according to the journey.

ROW TWO: Cie Generale des Ominbus of the 1920-1921 period, bus or tram, 2nd class 15c and 1st class 25c, both for more than one section

ROWS 3–5: These 7 tickets are all tram tickets from the CGPT, one of the 5 tram companies which combined with t he CGO to form the STCRP in 1921

(All tickets from the Malcolm Chase collection)

ABOVE: These 7 tickets are early STCRP issues from 1st January 1921 until the introduction of Klein Massot machines from 1927.
LEFT: Tramways Intra Muros tram ticket of probably the 1910 to 1921 period
lines 5/6 are all Klein massot machine tickets from the early 1930 to 1940, the latter having a year date in the printed text, issued by the STCR.

(All tickets from the Malcolm Chase collection)

BELOW: A selection of Klein massot machine tickets from the early 1930 to 1940, the latter having a year date in the printed text, issued by the STCRP.

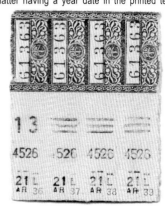

ABOVE: A 1930s selection

BELOW: 1937 series   1938 series   1940 series

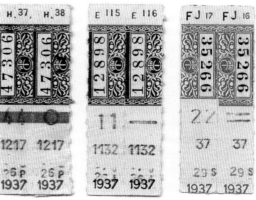

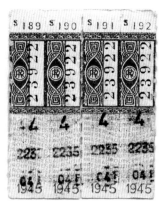   

ABOVE LEFT: Post Second World War – 1945 series. **ABOVE RIGHT:** 1947 series.

ABOVE and BELOW: These Klein massot machine tickets are STCRP issues above and RATP issues below. *(All tickets from the Malcolm Chase collection)*

BELOW LEFT: 1951 Tarif S. **BELOW and BELOW RIGHT:** 1957 Tarif T (same fares as Tarif S).

 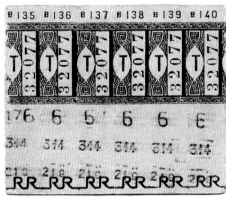 

BELOW: This green 20 is the reverse of a reduced fare Tickets Speciaux carnet for Mutiles de Guerre and Familles Nombreuses (war wounded and large families).

BELOW: Tarif Y – all 1967.

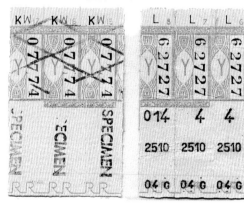  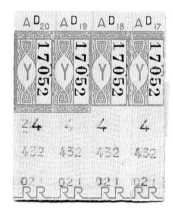 

ABOVE: Reverse of part of a tarif Y carnet.

BELOW: These white modern tickets are all driver issued tickets from 1973 onwards, not carnet tickets. One at least is issued through a Klein Massot machine; they were withdrawn in or just after 1973 and replaced by Camp BC 30 validators.

BELOW LEFT: 1973 – Tarif D – driver issue. **BELOW RIGHT:** 1973 – sans tafif.

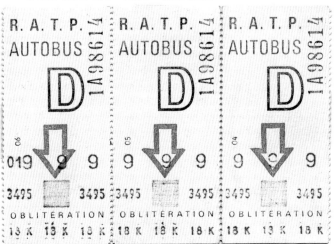 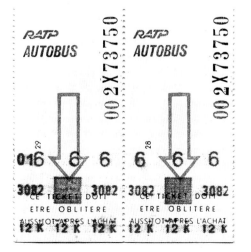 

54

YELLOW TICKETS: 1980s carnet issues valid on buses and the Metro.

LEFT: A special roll to celebrate 200th anniversary of the Revolution.

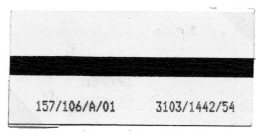

ABOVE: New green colour of carnetsintroduced March 1992.

ABOVE: Reverse of a standard carnet ticket but used on a suburban bus in 1990.

(All tickets from the Malcolm Chase collection except Mobilis which are from the Author's collection)

ABOVE: The Mobilis card was formerly used in conjunction with a Mobilis ticket and was personal to the holder (see reverse). It is no longer required, the ticket by iself being enough. That has still to be validated with date and user's name. *(Author's collection)*

RIGHT: The mauve ticket was in use from 1st January 2003 to 30th June 2007 only. The white ticket is the current one, from a carnet. It is the first ticket to carry the STIF name, in additon to that of RATP and SNCF. *(Author's collection)*

All tickets from the Malcolm Chase collection except Mobilis which are the Author's

Stopping Places and Shelters

Unless displaying the 'Complet' (full) sign, horse buses stopped on demand at any point along their line of route, with the exceptions already mentioned (*page 6*). Conductors, who normally travelled on the rear platform, were instructed to keep a sharp lookout for anyone who seemed to be hailing the vehicle. The only fixed stopping places were at the transfer stations, and these were announced by the conductor. These were quite large buildings, containing waiting rooms for passengers and an office for the 'controleur' (inspector). That officer gave arriving passengers a numbered boarding ticket and called out these numbers when the bus arrived. The stations had a prominent blue sign board with the CGO title in white letters. The horse trams seem to have had a more rigid system and generally only stopped at correspondance points. With the advent of mechanical traction, it was decided to change to a system of fixed stopping places for both buses and trams. The stop signs were usually affixed to street lamps.

At the same time a system of queue tickets was instituted, to allow an orderly system of boarding. Passengers took a ticket from a 'distributeur' mounted on the pole or lamp post and presented this to the conductor when the bus or tram arrived; they had no cash value and did not replace the normal travel tickets. Boarding could be a rather slow process, but this system did prevent arguments and was in marked contrast to the kind of free-for-all which prevailed in London until the second world war. The queue tickets also offered opportunities for a prank to local children, who would sometimes tear off three or four, then enjoy watching the conductor calling out these numbers for non-existent passengers. They lasted until the 1960s.

In 1922 the STCRP introduced the first free-standing stop signs, after careful consultation with the architects of both the Département and the municipal authorities. On top of these was mounted a panel, parallel to the street, listing the places served by the lines using the stop, and on the ends were two circular discs carrying the line letters. Request stops had green discs and fixed stops red discs. The distributor for queue tickets was mounted underneath. As gas lamps were progressively replaced by larger electric standards, individual stop signs became the norm and there were complaints from some quarters about this increase in street furniture. From 1945 all discs were red and yellow, with a diagonal division. They are now jade green, with the line numbers prominently mounted on panels with a colour corresponding to that of the line concerned.

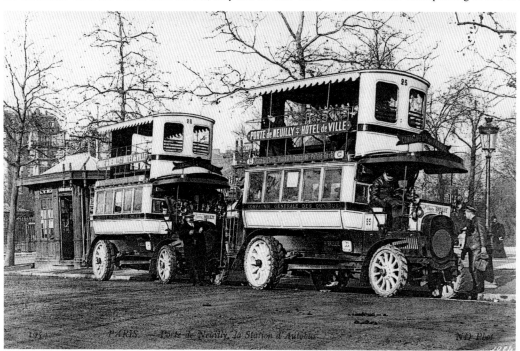

LEFT: The station at Porte de Neuilly can be seen to the left of the two P2 double-deckers, 25 and 26, awaiting departure on line C to Hôtel de Ville about 1908. *(Author's collection)*

BELOW: A present-day shelter, at the stop of Saint-Philippe-du-Roule in the rue de de Boethe, seen on 16th April 2008. *(Author)*

Liveries

The original vehicles of Baudry's Entreprise des Omnibus had a fairly simple livery of yellow below the waist and black above and, with some individual varieties, this was copied by most of his competitors. A few operators, such as the Citadines, varied this with a broad red band below the windows and, as a compliment to the reigning monarch (Charles X), the Carolines adopted blue and gold, the colours of the Bourbons. It is not known if they changed these after the revolution of 1830, but in any case the company went out of business in 1836. The Dames Réunies showed their individuality with a red livery and a broad green band, while one operator had this colour scheme in reverse. On its formation the CGO opted for a much more sober livery and its buses were either painted dark brown, or simply varnished – it is now not possible to say which. At a later date, probably around 1890, they changed to a brighter livery of yellow and, with the addition of a chocolate underframe and bonnet, this scheme was also carried by the P2 double-deckers.

The new single-deckers which appeared from 1911 onwards showed a complete break with the past, since they were painted green below the windows and cream above. The waist panels were lined in gold and the underframe, which was still chocolate, had red lining. With considerable simplification and the gradual omission of the lining, this livery lasted until the arrival of the first Standard buses in 1964. It was also used on the trolleybuses. The unsuccessful experiment with a red colour scheme has been mentioned. The livery worn by most of the new vehicles, and subsequently extended to those earlier models which still had some years to run, was a darker shade of green with off-white window surrounds and a green roof. On the double-deckers, this darker green was also used for the panels between the decks, although the prototype had much of this area painted green. Some suburban buses had green window surrounds with light green bands above and below, which gave them a distinctly Irish appearance! The Verney midibuses had a light blue and cream livery, similar to that of the new pneumatic-tyred trains on the Métro, but this did not spread to any other class in the fleet. The off-white later gave way to light grey and in this form this colour scheme lasted until the introduction of the SC10 R buses in 1980. On these, white replaced the light grey and was extended to cover most of the waist panel. Below this were bands of dark and light green and these were duplicated above the windows, while the roof was white. With the introduction of the RATP corporate livery in 1992, the basic colour scheme became white with a band of jade green above the windows and around the windscreen, with many but not all types also having a green band below the windows.

Although the RATP used a logo from its formation – the actual design being changed from time to time – none of these was used on the buses, except for the Verney midibuses, until the appearance of the current logo in 1992.

Preservation and the Centenary

Although the preservation movement got under way in Paris in 1957, with the foundation of the Association pour le Musée des Transports Urbains, Interurbains et Ruraux, its progress has been somewhat chequered.

The Association immediately set about building up a collection of road vehicles and, although many items of historic interest had already been scrapped, it had some success in forming a representative collection. The first home of this collection was in the former tram depot in Malakoff, to the south of the city. In 1973/4 the collection was moved to the former bus garage at Saint-Mandé, in the eastern suburbs, and there it remained until 1998, when this was closed. A new site was then found at Colombes, in the north-west, but due to the vagaries of local politics, the proposed museum did not open, save for some special days, and no work could be done to lay it out properly. Conservation work did, however, continue on individual vehicles. A new site has now been found in Chelles, to the north-east and situated on RER line E and this will open to the public in 2009. It is hoped that this will be the final move and that residents and visitors will at last have a proper chance to visit and admire this excellent collection.

There is a good selection of Paris buses in the collection. Some of these have been mentioned at the appropriate place in the fleet history, but a summary is given here.

Horse bus c1889 2177

Brillié-Schneider P2 20. This is an excellent reconstruction, rather than an original vehicle.

Schneider H 534

Renault PN 1347

Renault TN 4 B 1891

Renault TN 6 A 2515/63/73/2720

Renault TN 6 C1 one-man bus, 6284

Renault TN 6 C2 2728/59/88/2806/83

Renault TN 4 C 2963

Renault TN 4 F 3072/3/3132/3272

Renault TN 4 F as fitted for gas operation 3158

Renault TN 4 H-P 3488/4121

Renault TN 4 H-Bln .4133

LEFT: Renault TN6C2 no.2883 contrasts with Agora 2711 at Neuilly on 22 September 2002, while working a special service to Colombes museum. *(Author)*

Panhard K 63 D 4500
Somua OP 5/2 554 and 796
Somua OP5/3 365
Somua OP5/S283 1556
Chausson APU 1111
Chausson APVU4 1902
Verney midi-bus 4553
Standard buses PCMR 4375/4464
Standard PGR 2897/2900
Berliet double-decker 2204.
Standard buses SC 10 U-B 7269 and SC 10 R 3644.

A tower wagon of 1920, built on the chassis of a Renault H type bus.

One of the Vetra VBF trolleybuses has been preserved, but it wears Grenoble livery.

There are also many provincial buses and trolleybuses, as well as London RT2567 and London trolleybus no.796 and a good selection of carriages and taxis.

As the Paris trams had disappeared long before preservation was thought of, it was difficult to find any for the collection. However, two bogie motor cars of the CGO 500 class of 1907 were located at Hagondge and one (579) was donated by the mining company which had used it there. The other, no.589, originally went to the Belgian tramway museum group but was later given to the RATP, after full restoration and reversion to its original number of 505. It was planned

that this car would operate on line T1, for which purpose it was fitted with a pantograph, but sadly it was found that it was technically impossible to run it on the present-day system. A trailer of type ASL, no1630, was acquired form Marseille, to which city it had gone on the closure of the Paris system. There are also several trams from French provincial systems and a double-deck Standard car (488) from Glasgow.

The society has always worked closely with RATP and this was amply demonstrated during the celebrations of the centenary of the motorbus in Paris, which were actually held in October 2006, although the date fell four months earlier. An exhibition was held in Parc de la Villette during the week from 11th October and on Sunday 15th October, in fine autumnal weather, a parade of vintage and modern vehicles was held, starting from the Grand Palais and running to the Champ de Mars via the left bank of the Seine. After a pause, during which the vehicles could be admired, they returned to the starting point via the right bank. This was no mere running day for enthusiasts; ordinary Parisians turned out in their thousands and showed the degree of interest in public transport which is maintained by the citizens of the capital.

The RATP collection

The RATP itself has also preserved some historic vehicles. There are no fewer than 10 Renault TN 4 buses in its collection, renumbered into the 9xx series. Most of these are in running order and appear at open days. They are also available for private hire and are sometimes, like their present-day counterparts, used in films, such as *"C'est quoi ton petit boulot?"* (What's your little job?"), which was made in 1990,

starring Marléne Jobet, as well as various buses. While the buses have not appeared in as many films as have trains of the Métro, they have starred from time to time. In the Maison de la RATP at Bercy, there is among the other buses, a replica of an H class vehicle numbered 166. Bercy has also, from time to time, housed members of the AMTUIR collection, when the Association did not have adequate premises of its own.

Enthusiasts visiting Paris might like to know of two shops where transport books, videos and DVDs can be bought. One is the boutique of La Vie du Rail magazine. It is at 11 rue de Milan and can be reached by going up the rue d'Amsterdam from the east side of Saint-Lazare; the rue de Milan is on the right. Liège station on line 13 is also fairly near, in which case rue de Milan is on the left as you go down rue d'Amsterdam. It is open from Monday to Friday from 10 to 17hr. The other is the boutique "Objets du Patrimoine" which is maintained by the RATP and offers a wide selection of souvenirs as well as books and other items. It is located in the Salle des Echanges du RER in Châtelet les Halles station, near the stairs leading down to lines A and D. It is also open on Monday to Friday only, from 10 to 19hr. Its merchandise can be viewed on *www.souvenirs-metro.fr* and its postal address is 11, rue Pierre Lescot, Salle des Echanges du RER, Châtelet les Halles, 75001 Paris. There are also some bookshops with transport sections in the rue de Douai, near Pl Clichy.

LEFT: The horse bus awaiting restoration at Saint-Mandé in 1987. This view shows the amount of work which had to be undertaken to bring it to the standard shown in the earlier illustration. *(Author)*

ABOVE: The poster advertising the centenary. This example was at the Metro station Filles du Calvaire. *(Author)*

LEFT: Slightly hesitantly, Brillié-Schneider P2, No 20, leads the procession along the Quai d'Orsay. This replica PB2 was built on a Schneider H chassis from 1916 that had been used as a tractor at Championnet, using bits of a horse bus body that had been discovered in 1965 (the double-deckers did use former horse bus bodies, so that was a reasonable thing to do). The museum rebuilt the chassis and the mechanical units, while RATP renovated the body and put the whole lot together. *(Author)*

ABOVE: Along with PB2 534, the bus is surrounded by enthusiastic crowds after arrival at Champ de Mars. *(Author)*

BELOW: TN4H, 3488, leaves for the return journey. *(Author)*

ABOVE LEFT and RIGHT: Two of the floats, representing passengers of 1970 and 2000.

RIGHT: RATP operates four Scania high-specification coaches and in 2006 this one was the dedicated transport for France's first XV. It is outside the Petit Palais after the parade.

(All photographs by author)

BELOW: The line-up after arrival back at Ave Winston Churchill. First is Chausson 1111, then Standard 7269, double-decker 2204 and a Standard converted to a works vehicle.

LEFT: A preserved TN 4, renumbered to 901 and displaying a pre-1945 route letter indication, loads at the RATP headquarters for a round trip on Sunday 21st September 2008. *(Author)*

BELOW: A British built Leyland PDR1/1 demonstrator "awaiting the Judgement of Paris". In 1964, Leyland Motors repurchased this Alexander-bodied double-decker from Glasgow, where it had been LA91, to use as a demonstrator and sent it to Paris in the hope of breaking into the French market. No orders ensued. (*See page* 27) The scene is rue Lepic, just north of Blanche Metro station, near Pigalle. *(Leyland Publicity)*

Sightseeing

Clearly in a centre such as Paris, many buses were and are used on sightseeing duties and the full story of these would require a book in itself. At present the main services are provided by two operators, using open-top double-deckers. Les Cars Rouges, which is owned by the operator of the Versailles urban system SVTU and whose buses are (unsurprisingly) red, began operations in 1993 with ex-Wien Graf und Stift tri-axle double-deckers, of which here were ultimately 13. These were all withdrawn by 2000 and replaced by 14 Volvo B10M-62 vehicles (351-364), with East Lancashire bodies. These were followed between 2002 and 2005 by 14 Volvo B7L buses (365-377), with similar bodies. Nos.357-372 have bodies which can be fitted with a roof when necessary and in this guise, at least one, 357, has in recent years operated a city tour in Versailles. This runs as an ordinary service and Paris Mobilis tickets are valid on it. There are now also two Volvo B7 RLE buses, with bodywork of an unknown make. The other operator is L'Open Tour, which began in 1998 using two-axle Volvos with bodies by East Lancashire coachworks, of which there were twelve in all (01-12). Most have now been withdrawn. The next deliveries were of 16 tri-axle Neoplans (13-28) and there is also one Volvo B7 RLE. The services follow circular routes around the city centre and passengers can board and alight as often as they wish during the validity of their ticket. L'Open Tour uses a yellow livery. Fares in March 2008 were EUR22 for a two-day ticket with Les Cars Rouges and either EUR26 for a one-day ticket or EUR29 for a two-day ticket with L'Open Tour. While convenient and offering excellent views from the upper deck, and also a good way of orienting oneself if new to the city, the tours, it must be pointed out, are much dearer than normal RATP fares and are at the time of writing cost about five times the price of a Mobilis day ticket for two zones.

ONE OF SEBREE'S "SEEING PARIS" SIGHT-SKEING AUTOMOBILES
LEAVING THE AMERICAN EXPRESS CO.'S OFFICE, 11 RUE SCRIBE.

LEFT: An early sightseeing bus, about which nothing is known – although the service seems to have been aimed at visitors from the USA. *(Author's collection)*

BELOW: A curious double-decker Saviem operated by Paris-Vision, at Montmartre in April 1968. *(Author)*

ABOVE: By 1986, Paris Vision had a fleet of 3-axle Neoplan Skyliners operating its sightseeing service. *(Mike Davis)*

LEFT: In the 1990s, Les Cars Rouge began services with ex-Wien (Vienna) Graf und Stift double-deckers, one of which is seen at Trocadéro on 8th March 1995. *(Author)*

BELOW: Another ex-Vienna three-axle Graf und Stift seen five years later in 2000. The self-steering centremost axle and long rear overhang are evident in this view. *(Ron Phillips)*

RIGHT: One of the two-axle Volvos of L'Open Tour, at Madeleine in July 2000. *(Author)*

CENTRE: Porte de Bagnolet is not normally a tourist destination! This three-axle Neoplan of L'Open Tour is running back to its home depot of Les Lilas in April 2008. *(Author)*

BELOW: One of the Volvos of Les Cars Rouge approaches the Pont St-Michel on a wet day, 26th June 2006, with little demand for seats on the upper deck. *(Author)*

Foreign buses in Paris

LEFT: During the 1970s and 80s, Top Deck Travel ran numerous British-built Bristol double-decker buses throughout Europe, North Africa and Asia. They were frequently seen in Paris where Bristol Lodekka YHT 932 is seen amid tourist vehicles in August 1979. To the right is a Saviem Paris-Vision sightseeing coach with short upper-deck. To the left of the Bristol is a French registered Mercedes-Benz touring coach belonging to Wahl, while behind it is another Mercedes-Benz, this time a West German registered touring coach. *(Mike Davis)*

RIGHT: This visitor was from the former West Berlin fleet of BVG and is an MAN BüD2U 63, still carrying its former owner's fleet number 1564. It was parked on Boulevarde Rochechouart in August 1986. The operator, Jörg Hoffmann and Klaus Schauerte, was the German equivalent of Top Deck Travel, catering for the Australian market, thus the tour name is in English – or Australian. *(Mike Davis)*

BELOW: By July 1985, Top Deck Travel were operating this later model Bristol FLF Lodekka (JAE 632D), as well as the older LD type parked behind it at Île de la Cité, nearby the Cathedral of Notre Dame. Conversion of the upper deck for use as sleeping accommodation can be seen in the form of curtains, also useful in hot climates as protection from the sun. *(Mike Davis)*

RIGHT: Rear views are rare and this vehicle is indeed rare. It is a Leyland Royal Tiger Worldmaster LERT1/1 with Weymann Arcadian 40-seat centre entrance coach body. The operator is Autocares SAMAR of Madrid and the vehicle carried Spanish registration M.236363 when seen here in September 1963. *(Ron Phillips collection)*

RIGHT: The Mercedes-Benz O305 VöV on the left, 6393 JR94, was second-hand from a West German operator and in 1985 was being used as a shuttle bus between a camp site in the Bois de Boulogne and the Metro station at Porte Maillot. *(Mike Davis)*

RIGHT: British coaches carrying school parties are frequently seen in Paris. Here an unusual 4 metre high double deck Plaxton bodied coach waits at the Notre Dame coach parking area. *(Ron Phillips)*

Paris buses have also travelled abroad

Many RATP buses have seen further service in Francophone parts of the World as well as other places, such as Albania. Also preserved and serving members of the fleet can be seen outside France – a few examples of the latter are shown below.

LEFT: A British preserved Renault TN4H climbs away from the sea front at Brighton, after taking part in the HCVC rally in the early 1970s. *(Author)*

BELOW: A TN4, 3047, is in very active preservation in Leipzig. At Hauptbahnhof in June 2006 it awaits its next run on sightseeing duty in company of an ex-Berlin SD class double-decker. *(Author)*

LEFT: In June 1997 the 150th anniversary of Berlin buses was celebrated and many other operators sent buses to the city to work on normal services for a week. Most came from other German cities, but Agora 2092 was from Paris and is seen here at the Prenzlauerberg (Michael Angelostrasse) terminus of line 100, along with BVG low-floor double-decker 3021. *(Author)*

Trams of Paris

Unlike that of the bus, the history of the tram in Paris is extremely complex and no more than a summary can be given within the context of a book of this type.

The first horse tram line to open was instituted by a French engineer Alphonse Loubat, who had worked on the tramways in New York city in the early 1850s and who brought the idea to Paris in 1853. He obtained authorisation to construct a trial line between Passy and Place de la Concorde, then onwards via the Cours de la Reine to terminate at Louvre. This worked successfully and on 18 February 1854 he was authorised by decree of Napoléon III to construct and work, at his own cost and risk, a line between Vincennes and Sèvres, with a branch to the suburb of Boulogne. However, there was concern that such a line would cause congestion in the narrow rue du Faubourg-Saint-Antoine and might also interfere with traffic to the imperial court on the Quai des Tuileries and, as actually built, the line was limited to a short stretch between Rond-Point de Boulogne and Pont de l'Alma. This opened in September 1855 and a second, suburban line was then opened between Pont Marly and Rueil station.

With the creation of the CGO in 1854, Loubat was put under some pressure to cede his concession to the new company and it was handed over on 15th September 1856. However, he went on to open a new line from Sèvres to Versailles on 10th November 1857, while on the same day the CGO opened a link from Porte de Saint-Cloud to Sèvres. Through services were begun and in 1866 these were prolonged to Louvre, using cars which could also operate on road surfaces without rails. The actual means by which this was done is not known. In 1873 this method of working was replaced by a normal tram line.

The traffic generated by the exposition of 1867, which attracted eleven million visitors, showed up all too clearly the drawbacks of the horse buses and there was pressure to extend the rail-based system. Development was held up by the Franco-Prussian war of 1870-71 and the following troubles of the Commune, but in 1872 it was decided to set up a commission to consider the question more closely and this reported favourably in 1873. It recommended that a network of tramways should be set up under the auspices of the Département of the Seine, but worked by one or more private companies. There should be a circular line around the outer city and ten suburban lines, which would penetrate into central Paris. This plan was given official approval by a decree signed by President MacMahon on 9th August 1873, but with the modification that the circular line and all lines within the city should be worked by the CGO. The suburban lines would be worked by two companies, the Tramways Nord and Sud (North and South), these paying a rental to the CGO for the use of the tracks within Paris. The TN opened its first line on 3rd September 1874, the CGO on 18th June 1875 and the TS on 3rd November 1875. In 1875 also a new line, not part of the above scheme, was constructed by the CGO between Louvre and Vincennes.

The new system met with great approval from the travelling public and by 1879 the CGO was working a network of 16 lines. As with buses, these were designated by letters, but to avoid confusion with the former, these were prefixed by T. Thus line TC was Louvre – Vincennes. The other two companies each had eleven lines. However, all was not well financially with the two suburban companies and both declared themselves bankrupt in 1884. After some delay, they were reconstituted as the Tramways de Paris et du Département de la Seine (TPDS) and the Compagnie Générale Parisienne des Tramways (CGPT) respectively. Later other companies appeared on the scene, some quite small, such as the Chemin de Fer du Bois de Boulogne, which had one line serving the park of its title, others, such as the Chemins de Fer Nogentais, rather larger, with nine lines in the outer western suburbs by 1900. By that year there were 13 companies providing tram services in and around Paris and some of these competed with the lines of the CGO on certain sections within Paris. By 1890 the CGO had 17 lines in service, the TPDS 16 and the CGPT eleven. In the 1890s these totals were increased by five, three and two new lines respectively. There were some steam-worked lines serving outer suburbs, but the steam tram as known in Britain was tried only briefly within central Paris. There was also a cable tram line from Pl de la République to Belleville, which was known as a funicular, but was in fact a conventional cable line as can still be found in San Francisco.

As, by 1900, its concession had only ten years to run, the CGO was not willing to invest in mechanisation by conventional methods and instead chose to place in service a variety of mechanically-propelled cars, powered variously by compressed air, steam and accumulators. Some lines, however, remained with horse power. Although electricity was one of the main themes of the 1900 exposition, this could not hide the fact that Paris was lagging far behind other large cities in its application to urban transport ; in the following year, when Glasgow in turn hosted an international exhibition, it showed just what could be done with an efficient, modern tramway system, electrified on the overhead line principle.

After a good deal of hesitation, it was decided to reform the system completely when the concessions of the three major companies expired in 1910. This was duly carried into effect and the number of companies was reduced to nine. There was also a good deal of harmonisation of working practices and fares. The CGO was to electrify its system without delay. It did so, with impressive speed and efficiency, and the last horse tram ran in 1913, while the last of its mechanical marvels came out of service days before the outbreak of the first world war. Within central Paris, much use was made of conduit track, to avoid overhead wires. The new system worked well and passenger numbers increased from 339 million in 1909 to 490 million in 1913, but the new equilibrium was wrecked by the consequences of the war and by 1920 a new solution had to be found. As related in the history of the bus system, this was the creation of the STCRP in 1921, which ultimately brought all the tramways in and around Paris under unified control.

In the early 1920s the new management made many improvements to the tram system, which now comprised 112 lines, rising to 122 in 1925, with 1,111 track kilometres. However, anti-tram feelings emerged in Paris rather sooner and rather more strongly than in other comparable cities and the authorities ultimately forced a policy of total abandonment on a rather unwilling STCRP. The development of the Renault TN 4 bus *(q.v.)* provided a vehicle which could reasonably match the capacity of a tram and its arrival sounded the death knell of the Paris tram. The last ran within the city on 15 March 1937 and the last in the suburbs on 14th August 1938. Only about a dozen people turned out to mark its passing.

RIGHT: A 200 class double-decker (220) of the CGPT working on the overhead system, stands at Malakoff terminus in the southern suburbs, preparatory to returning to Saint-Germain-des-Près on line 13. This must have been a short working, since this service normally ran through to Les Halles. These trams, on maximum traction bogies, were built in 1901 and, at the time that this photograph was taken, this one would have completed its journey using accumulators. In 1911 this practice was discontinued and the trams were fitted with equipment for conduit operation within Paris. *(Author's collection)*

1602. MALAKOFF
Route de Châtillon - Station des Tramways - G. I.

The Tram Fleets

As stated above, Paris trams of the first generation were a varied lot! The horse trams were generally double-deckers and mostly single-ended. As a result they looked much more like their contemporaries in the bus fleet than was the case in Britain and Ireland. The mechanically-powered trams with which the CGO replaced them were also double-deckers and also single-ended. The upper deck was sheltered by a light roof and a windscreen, but open at the sides. In service, these normally pulled a double-deck trailer, converted from a horse car. The three other main operators ran a variety of trams which used battery power, a combination of that and conventional electric power or, in the case of the Nogentais company, the latter alone. The steam tram lines used small locomotives, pulling several trailer cars, generally of single-deck layout, and the Belleville cable line used single-deckers. For its main electrification, the CGO opted for central-entrance single-deckers and this type was copied, with improvements, by the STCRP.

20 PARIS. La Place Saint-Michel et Notre-Dame. — ND Phot.

62 - PARIS. — La Station des Tramways de Passy Hôtel de Ville et la Gare de Passy

F. F. PARIS

ABOVE RIGHT: This scene at Pl Saint-Michel about 1900 illustrates the variety of forms of tram used in Paris at the time. Crossing the bridge are two vehicles of the CGO – that on the left is a horse bus, while the similar but larger vehicle on the right is a tram of the 50-seater type, first introduced in 1878, when the design won a gold medal at the exposition of that year. It is on line TAH, Gare du Nord – Bd de Vaugirard, which remained worked by horse power until the general electrification. In the centre of the photograph is a class C single-decker of the Est Parisien company. As this line was at that time electrified on the Diatto system of contact studs, the trolley has been tied down. The tram is most probably running on line 7, Bonneuil-Concorde, the latter terminus being in fact on the left bank and, strictly speaking, not at Concorde. A CGO horse bus is coming in on the right. *(Author's collection)*

CENTRE RIGHT: Two compressed-air cars of the CGO, nos.62 (left) and 64, working on line TJ, Passy – Hôtel de Ville and seen at the former point. The trams' air reservoirs were topped up at this terminus and one of the crew can be seen preparing to connect a hose pipe to car 64. Coke and water were also taken on board. The CGO first experimented with this form of traction in 1894, but these cars, of which there were 148, dated from 1900; they ran until August 1914. *(Author's collection)*

RIGHT: Steam tram 717, powered by the Purrey system, running on line TL, Bastille – Porte Rapp on the Boulevard Saint-Germain. The first of these trams went into service on 17th September 1900 and they were the most successful of all the various forms of mechanical traction tried by the CGO. Ultimately there were 50 double-deckers and 36 single-deckers and the last ran on 13th June 1914. *(Author's collection)*

2149. — LES MOYENS DE TRANSPORT A PARIS — Tramway à vapeur, système V. Purrey (Cie Générale des Omnibus)

RIGHT: The Belleville cable tramway ran for just over 2km from the east side of Place de la République to Belleville. It was of metre gauge and was opened for traffic on 25 August 1891. In this view the tram appears to be a centre-entrance vehicle, but it was in fact made up by joining two of the original very small cars, using one platform of one of these. There were 21 of these trams and they continued in service until replaced by bus line BF on 18 July 1924. A cyclist is enjoying an easy ride uphill. *(Author's collection)*

CENTRE RIGHT: A two-axle double-deck car of the Chemins de fer Nogentais, on a line serving the western suburbs, from the Porte de Vincennes terminus of Métro line 1. These trams entered service in August 1900, replacing compressed-air cars and, unusually for Paris trams of that time, were equipped only to operate on the overhead line system.. The top decks were later enclosed and these were the last double-deck trams to run in Paris, being withdrawn in 1929. *(Author's collection)*

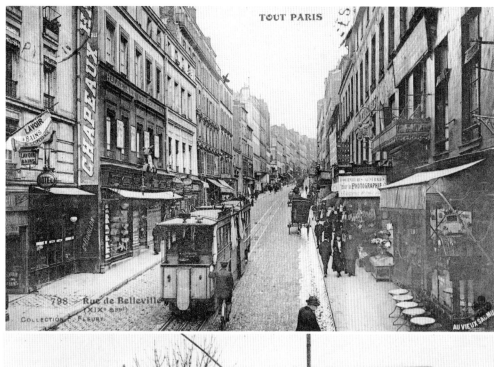

LEFT: A busy scene in the rue du Louvre, on the approach to the terminus at Louvre in STCRP days, probably about 1928. Four services used this particular terminal point and all trams are running on the conduit system. On the left are two two-axle L class motor cars, working on line 13A, Créteil-Charenton-Louvre, that on the inner track pulling an A class bogie trailer. On the right another L class car with an A class trailer approaches on line 3 from Vincennes. The L class was developed by the STCRP in 1923 and was of advanced design for the period, but its lightweight construction gave problems in service and several modifications had to be carried out after the type had been in service for some years. The bogie trailers of class A were originally developed by the CGO in 1912 but many more were built by the STCRP and the class ultimately numbered 394. Many were fitted with a driving position and were used with motor cars of classes G and L to form *'rames reversibles'* (reversible sets) *(Author's collection)*

71

Modern Tramways in Paris

The present system consists of four separate lines, which are not at present physically connected. These are:-

T1 Saint-Denis – Noisy-le-Sec
T2 Issy Val-de-Seine – La Défense
T3 Pont de Gariglliano – Porte d'Ivry
T4 Bondy – Aulnay-sous-Bois. (This line is operated by SNCF)

Although the revival of the tram in France dates back to 1975, it was some time before serious consideration was given to introducing it in the capital. It was first suggested for what is now line T1 in a report in 1977, but this did not lead to anything at the time, as the RATP saw bus corridors as the answer to the heavier flows of traffic on surface lines. However the idea was taken up with enthusiasm by the Council of Saint-Denis and in due course this body managed to convince the RATP that a tram line along the road numbered RN186 between the centre of Saint-Denis and Bobigny would be a viable proposition. On 28th October 1983 it was adopted by the RATP board, this being followed in April 1984 by agreement of the STP. A public enquiry was then held and a declaration of public utility obtained on 19th December 1984. However, other administrative problems then arose with the Region of Ile-de-France and work did not begin until April 1989. As was to be the case with line T3 later, local authorities seized the opportunity to carry out much urban regeneration along the route while the line was being built. It was finally opened from Bobigny (Pablo Picasso) to La Courneuve on 6th July 1992 and on to Saint-Denis on 21th December of the same year. At the eastern end, an extension from Bobigny to Noisy-le-Sec was opened on 15th December 2003.

Line T1 – Saint-Denis–Noisy-le-Sec

To-day line T1 is just exactly 12km long and has 25 stops, of which five provide interchange with either the Métro or the RER and suburban railways. With the former there are interchange points at Bobigny (line 5), la Courneuve (line 7) and Saint-Denis (line 13), while with the RER and the Transilien suburban lines there is easy interchange at Noisy (line E) and, with a short walk, at Saint-Denis (line B). Almost all the track is on street, but is segregated from other traffic. The cars are shedded at Bobigny, where they share a depot and workshops with the trains of line 5.

Line T1 uses only trams of the French standard design developed by what was then GEC-Alsthom and first placed in service in Grenoble in 1987. These are partly low-floor vehicles, with raised sections over the end bogies. The original fleet, numbered 101-119, soon proved to be insufficient for the traffic offering and additional trams were required for the Noisy extension. This need was met by transferring 16 trams of the same design from line T2, where they were replaced by new Citadis cars.

This line has been brilliantly successful in attracting passengers. In a poll organised in February 2003, riders commented that it was *"Le Mode de Transport idéal"* and that it also was *"Agréable comme le bus et efficace comme le Métro."* (as pleasant as the bus and as efficient as the Métro). When the original line was planned it was estimated that it might attract a daily ridership of 55,000. In 2006, after the opening of the extension to Noisy, it carried 100,000 per working day, or 29.9 million annually. This is no doubt partly due to the greatly increased average speed over the buses which it replaced, 17km/hr as against 11km/hr. Traffic is heavy throughout the day and is well balanced in both directions.

Two extensions are currently planned. In the west, work is now under way on a 4.9km extension to Asnières-Gennevilliers. This section will incorporate some mixed running with general traffic, with priority measures for the trams. There will be interchange with RER line C at Gennevilliers and, when it is extended, with line 13 of the Métro. This extension should open at the end of 2011. At a later date, the line will be extended to Colombes SNCF station and Rueil-Malmaison, although the latter section may at first be served by a busway. From Noisy an extension of 8km to Montreuil and Val-de-Fontenay is planned but was for a long time blocked by local opposition. This has now been resolved but planning has to begin again and it is unlikely that this line could open before 2015.

As it proved to be impossible to run any preserved French trams on this line, a two-axle M class car was acquired from Vienna and is now available for private hire.

French standard tram as used on line T1
Length 29.4m, width 2.3m, 4 x 110kW motors, 174 passengers, 52 seated

BELOW: No.107 of line T1 at Bobigny (Pablo Picasso) on 5th March 1995. This shows the original livery carried by this class. *(Author)*

ABOVE: A driver's eye view of the interchange with the Métro at la Courneuve on T1. Car 101 advances towards Saint-Denis. *(Author)*

BELOW: Stations on T1 are neat and fit in well with the urban landscape, the trams and other road traffic have been accommodated is such a way as that both run side by side neatly but without conflict. This is Danton, looking west towards Saint-Denis, in 1997. *(Author)*

Line T2 – Tramway du Val-de-Seine

Line T2 differs from T1 in almost every respect. For most of its length it runs on the trackbed of a former suburban railway line, opened to the public from Issy-les-Moulineaux to Puteaux on 1st May 1889, the year of another international exposition, which it was designed to serve. It was electrified on the 650V DC third rail system on 22 July 1928. Traffic was not at any time heavy and declined gradually over the years until the line was carrying no more than 5,000 passengers per day in 1983. It was not converted to AC overhead when other lines in the western suburbs were so treated in the 1980s and some converted stock dating from 1951 rather erratically kept the service going while the authorities debated on its future. There was general agreement that a modern tramway was likely to be the best method of modernising the line, extending it at the same time to La Défense, the latter section being built on railway-owned land. A declaration of public utility was obtained on 18th March 1993 and work began on the conversion. The track was completely replaced by welded rail (still to railway profile), overhead line was erected, station platforms were lowered and several level crossings were closed. At Issy-les-Moullineaux a metal viaduct was replaced by one in reinforced concrete. Construction at the north end was delayed by an action brought by the mayor of Puteaux, who tried to claim compensation for alleged nuisance to be caused by the tramway, but this was finally dismissed and the line was formally opened throughout on 1st July 1997. Unlike the former trains, the trams run on the right. There is interchange with line C of the RER at Issy Val-de-Seine, with line A and Métro line 1 at La Défense and with suburban trains both there and at Puteaux..

Line T2 was an instant success and by March 1998 was carrying 35,000 passengers per day. By 2006 this figure had increased to 80,000 on week-days. An extension of 2.3km from Issy Val-de-Seine to Porte de Versailles is now under construction and should open in December 2009. This will have interchange with Métro lines 8 at Pl Balard and 12 at Porte de Versailles and it will also meet line T3 at the latter point, although through running will not be possible due to the difference in wheel profile. At the north end, the line will be extended by 4.2km in 2011 to Bezons, with seven new stations.

The line was initially worked by 16 trams of the type used on T1 (201-216), but with railway-profile wheels. These were later transferred to augment those on T1 and T2 is now worked by 26 trams, numbered 401-426, of the Citadis 302 design, built by what is now Alsthom in 2002/3. These are five-section cars, with a low floor throughout and are fitted with multiple-unit equipment. With the growth of traffic, many workings now use coupled cars. The control centre, depot and workshops are located at Issy-les-Moulineaux. This has a capacity for 32 trams, to cater for future growth of the fleet.

Visitors should note that, although line T2 begins and ends in fare Zone 2, it passes en route through Zone 3 and passengers travelling from end to end of the line should have a ticket valid for that zone.

ABOVE: Many parts of line T2 are quite scenic, especially where it runs alongside the Seine. This view near Parc de Saint-Cloud, shows No 213, one of the trams built for this line, but since transferred to Line 1, en route to La Défense in September 1998. (Author)

BELOW: A coupled set of Citadis trams, led by No 413, reversing at Issy Val-de-Seine on line T2 on 11th January 2008. They are using the first part of the extension to Porte de Versailles. (Author)

Citadis 302 – line T2
Length 32.2m, width 2.4, 4 x 140kW motors, 213 passengers, 48 seated

Line T3 – *Tramway des Maréchaux Sud*

This line differs again from those described above. It is so called since it runs along the southern boulevards which are all are named after former marshals in the French army.

In the section dealing with the history of the bus services, mention was made of the former passenger service on the Petite Ceinture circular railway line, which was replaced by buses in 1934. As traffic increased on the roads and as passenger numbers also increased, the bus service became overcrowded and also at times erratic. By 1993 line PC was transporting 130,000 passengers per day. In that year, when the extension of T2 to Porte de Versailles was first mooted, the RATP suggested that this should be further extended to Porte d'Ivry, along the line of part of the PC bus service. The authorities generally supported the idea, but there was considerable debate about whether this line should use the trackbed of the former railway, which now saw little traffic, or whether it should be on the series of roads known from their names as the Boulevards des Maréchaux. Use of the railway formation would allow a fairly high speed (28km/hr) but interchange with the Métro would not be easy and a great deal of money would have to be spent to make the stations fully accessible. Placing the line on the highway would cost slightly more and would result in a lower service speed, but access and interchange would be much easier and it was calculated that more passengers would be attracted to it than if it were on the railway formation. Additionally, placing it on street would allow the local authorities to carry out various schemes of urban improvement and introduce traffic management to reduce the volume of motor vehicles using these roads and so improve the quality of life for residents of the area. The debate went on for some time and became fairly acrimonious but after the local elections of 2001, it was decided to adopt the street running solution. However, the line was now envisaged as a self-contained operation, rather than as part of T2. Work began in 2003 and the line was opened throughout on 16th December 2006. This brought the tram back in to the city area of Paris after an absence of over 68 years.

Line T3 is at present 7.9km long and runs on reserved track, on the highway, from Pont de Garliagno in the west to Porte d'Ivry in the south-east. There are 17 stops, including the termini, of which six provide interchange with the Métro and two with the RER. The depot, workshops and control centre are situated on a short spur from Place Balard in the rue du Général Lucotte. To date the traffic on the line has exceeded all expectations, to the extent that the millionth passenger arrived long before the RATP was ready to welcome him/her! In its first complete year of operation the line carried 25 million passengers, an increase of more than 50% over the total carried by the PC bus service over the same length.

Service is provided by a fleet of 21 trams of Alstom's Citadis 402 type, numbered 301-321. These are seven-section cars, with 100% low floor configuration.

There are ambitious plans to extend this line. In the west, it is proposed to prolong it by about 2.5km to Porte d'Auteuil station (Line 10), but the exact line of route has not been finalised and, following the municipal elections of 2008, this extension now seems less likely. However, in the east much greater things are planned. Construction of an extension to Porte de Charenton has now begun and it is planned that the line will be extended from there right round the eastern side of the city to Porte de la Chapelle in the north, thus recreating more than half of the Petite Ceinture railway line. This new section would provide interchange with no fewer than eight Métro lines, as well as RER lines C and A. A public enquiry on this further extension began in May 2008.

Citadis 402 – line T3
Length 43.7m, width 2.65m, 6 x120kW motors, 304 passengers, 78 seated

> **FARES:** The fare system and control of the service on lines T1-T3 are as for the road services.

BELOW: No 311 of line T3 at Porte de Versailles on 11th January 2008. *(Author)*

Line T4 – La ligne des Coquetiers

Aulnay-sous-Bois – Bondy

Just as was the case a century ago, the Paris tramways of today show a great deal of variety.

This line in the eastern suburbs also replaces a railway service, of which the first section opened to traffic in 1875. Its name of "la Ligne des Coquetiers" (the Eggcup Line) recalls the agricultural nature of the area when it was built. It is totally different in history and present-day operation from the three lines already described. It was worked more as a tramway than a railway line and as urban growth reached out to the area it served, it became virtually a tramway on reserved track in the middle of suburban streets. A large number of level crossings hindered operation and caused considerable problems for motorists. The southern section form Bondy to Gargan was electrified at 25kV AC in May 1962 but the portion from that point to Aulnay was not electrified until September 1977. Latterly the line was worked by electric locomotives of class BB16500, pulling or pushing sets of stainless steel suburban stock. As the northern part remained single track, headways were poor and passenger numbers declined, to under 10,000 per day by 2000. The fall in traffic was particularly marked after the cessation of through services to the Gare de l'Est in 1999.

In 2000 it was decided to replace the trains by trams and to upgrade the line. The northern section was given double track – necessitating the construction of a new viaduct over RN 3 at Gargan – and the level crossings were converted to normal road intersections with colour light signalling and three new halts were built. The trains ran for the last time on 14th December 2003 and the line re-opened as a tramway on 18th November 2006. Service has been much improved to give a six minute frequency at peak times.

The line remains in the hands of SNCF and is now worked by 15 Avanto tram-trains built by Siemens. These are the first tram-trains to run in France and the only trams anywhere to use 25kV AC. They are dual-voltage but at present the facility to change to 750V DC is not used. Maximum speed is 100km/hr but this is attained only when running on the main line to and from the depot. On line T4 the maximum is 70km/hr, but this is seldom attained, mainly due to the need to slow down for road crossings. These trams carry two fleet numbers, one being an SNCF rolling stock number and the other a simple fleet number, prefixed by the letters TT, (TT01-15). Within each tram each section has its own SNCF carriage number ; thus in TT01, the numbers run 25501 25101 25201 25301 25502. Clearly these fine trams, with a capability to run at 70km/hr on the main line, might be considered extravagant for a short line of this nature, but there are plans for extensions at each end and the operator no doubt wished to gain experience of operating this type of car before embarking on schemes elsewhere in France. The trams are shedded and maintained at the main line depot at Noisy-le-Sec.

Note: At present the Ticket+ is not valid on this line, but this may change later in 2008.

Siemens Avanto - Line T4
Length 36.7m, width 2.65m, 4 x 200kW motors, 242 passengers, 80 seated

ABOVE: A scene on line T4, with car T10, on the Boulevard Pasteur between Allée de la Tour Rendez-Vous and Pavillons-sous-Bois on 10th March 2007. (Author)

RIGHT: On the same day, car 01 awaits departure form Bondy terminus, where there is same-level interchange with outbound trains on RER line E. (Author)

ABOVE: Tram TT05 at Allée de la Tour Rendez-Vous on 10th March 2007. *(Author)*

Possible future tram lines.

Apart from the extensions of existing lines, there are currently plans for various other new tram lines in Ile de France.

1 A short line of 4km from Meudon to Boulogne/Saint-Cloud. This may be ready by 2012. However, the mayor for the area, elected in 2008, is firmly against the scheme and it may not go ahead.

2 A line in the south-west from Châtillon to Viroflay. This will be worked by rubber-tyred vehicles on the Translohr system, as running in Clermont-Ferrand, and will incorporate a tunnel section. Work has now begun and the line should open to Vélizy by the end of 2011 and on to Viroflay by 2012.

3 A line of 11km from Villejuif to Athis-Mons via Orly, which is planned to open in 2012. It may later be extended to Juvisy and should relieve bus line 183, which runs on a similar course on roads to the east, of some of its traffic.

4 Two short lines, totalling 9.25km in all, from Saint-Denis northwards to Epinay and Villetaneuse, with 17 stations. This scheme was approved by the board of RATP on 8 February 2008 and the lines may be in service by 2013. They will require 20 trams.

5 A line around Paris to link most of the terminal stations and replace bus line 91. The mayor of Paris is in favour of this plan, but no detailed studies have as yet been carried out.

6 A line from Saint-Denis to Garges-Sarcelles has also been approved and this will also be served by a rubber-tyred tramway. It will be 6.6km long and will open for traffic in 2011.

7 In July 2008 plans were announced in the context of Plan Espoir Banlieue (A Plan to bring hope to the suburbs), for a line extending line T4 by 5.8km via Le Raincy to Clichy-sous-Bois and Montfermeuil. As an instrument of urban regeneration, this will be financed by the French government.

8 Under the same scheme, a tram-train line is planned from Massy-Palaiseau to Evry and Epinay-sur-Orge, using the tracks of the Grande Ceinture railway line as far as Evry. The first section will replace part of RER line C and the line will then operate as a conventional tramway to Epinay. A westward extension from Massy to Versailles may follow in 2015.

9 Another tram-train service will by 2015 work what is known as the Tangentielle Ouest (Western Tangent). It will run from Achère-Ville (RER line A) via Boissy-le-Roi to Saint-Cyr, to the west of Versailles (RER line C), with a branch to Saint-Germain-en-Laye and the Saint-Germain terminus of RER line A. The section for Saint-Germain to Saint-Cyr is likely to be opened first.

These last three lines will use Alsthom Dualis vehicles, for which an order was placed in 2007.

The Montmartre Funicular

While most visitors to Paris will be unaware of the growing tramway network, despite the impressive number of passengers it carries, almost all will know the short funicular line which links lower Montmartre to the church known as the Basilique du Sacré Coeur (Basilica of the Sacred Heart) and to a view point which gives an excellent panorama over the city centre. This carries only 0.01% of all RATP traffic, but has over the years been appreciated by thousands who have been spared the climb up the steep flight of 222 stone steps.

Montmartre, to the north of the city centre, has for centuries been associated both with religion and with tourism. In 1873 construction of the basilica began and the number of visitors to the area increased considerably as it took shape, but the aforementioned steps were a deterrent for many. In 1899 the City Council decided to build a funicular railway between place Saint-Pierre and the rue Lamarck, adjacent to the church. Construction began almost immediately and the line was opened for traffic on 12th July 1900. As built the line was a double-track counterbalance funicular, 102.8m in length, with a difference in height between the lower and upper stations of 37m, giving a gradient of 37%. It was operated by water power. The two cars could each carry 48 passengers, in four stepped compartments, and stations had stepped platforms to fit these. A brakesman rode on the upper platform of each to apply the service brake. A Strub rack rail provided for emergency braking. Journey time was 70 seconds and the fares were 10 centimes up and 5 centimes down, with workmen's fare of five centimes. The line was successful and was soon carrying about one million passengers annually. It was operated by its builders, the Société Nouvelle des Établissements Decauville, on a thirty-year concession.

ABOVE: The line as originally operated. At the lower station, carriages pulled by goats offer some competition! *(Author's collection)*

When the concession expired in 1931, the line closed for modernisation and it re-opened on 2nd February 1935. It now used electric power and the new cars, which could carry 50, had flat floors, stations being rebuilt to suit these. The journey time remained 70 seconds. It was now part of the STCRP system and the fare was a one-section ticket for the bus service. At some date in the 1940s, probably on the formation of the RATP, operation was transferred to line 2 of the Métro and the fare became one ticket for that system. In 1962 the line was closed for a few months to allow modernisation of the electrical supply system and the RATP took advantage of this to replace the cabins by new ones with aluminium bodies and to improve the stations.

For many years the number of passengers remained fairly steady, with a gradual increase to about 1.5m annually. From 1975 onwards there was a remarkable growth and for the first time, the number using the line in each direction was virtually the same. This was mainly due to parking difficulties in Montmartre. By 1989 the line was carrying 2.35m annually. This led to problems at peak times – the beginning and end of the tourist day and the times of services in the basilica – and the RATP decided that a second total modernisation was required to enable the line to cope with these numbers efficiently. It closed again on 30th September 1990 and re-opened on 4th October 1991. Shortly before that, it starred in its first film, "Les Ripoux" (The Crooks), in 1989.

The line is now a funicular in name only. Its technology is that of two cable-operated lifts working independently on inclined planes and it is thus possible at quiet times to have only one cabin in service. Stations now have platform doors, synchronised with the arrival and departure of the cabins. Operating speed has been increased to 3.5m/second and journey time is 40 seconds. Operation is entirely automatic and only two members of staff are now required, both based in the lower station. All nine staff who work on the line have been given a course in English! The cabins are of a more attractive, rounded appearance than their predecessors and can carry 60 passengers. Taken together, these improvements have increased hourly capacity to 2,000 passengers per direction, as against 1,000 previously carried.

On 7th December 2006 the line experienced its first accident, fortunately without injury to anyone. During trials of the braking systems, a cable broke and a cabin made a very rapid descent to the lower station, being badly damaged when it reached the end of the line. After a thorough investigation, and much to the relief of visitors, the Ministry allowed the resumption of a partial service, using the non-damaged cabin, on 30th June 2007. Full service resumed later in that year.

LEFT: The 1935 cars seen here towards the lower left of this general view of the Basilica. This generation of cars carried the legend 'Funiculaire de Montmartre ' on the skirt panels beneath the front windows, which were divided. The cars carried the green and cream livery of the STCRP buses and trams. *(Commercial postcard Ron Phillips collection)*

LEFT: Looking up at the upper station with a 1962 car in the platform. *(Author)*

ABOVE: One of the 1962 cabins, seen in 1986. By this time the only inscription on the front skirt panels was graffiti. *(Mike Davis)*

LEFT: The present system from a similar viewpoint to that above left. The modernisation of 1990/91 involved the rebuilding of both the upper and lower station buildings, although each was to a different design *(Author)*

LEFT: A heavily laden car of the 1990 type, probably – judging by the attitude of the passengers – descending. The lower car is stood at the station as each cabin is operated separately, according to demand. *(Ron Phillips)*

Extracts from a 1900s Tram and Buys Map

NOMENCLATURE DES LIGNES D'AUTOBUS

C. Neuilly (par l'Av. du Roule), Porte de Neuilly-Hôtel-de-Ville.
J. St-Ouen (Marie)-Place St-Michel.
L. St-Ouen (Bd. V.-Hugo)-Filles-du-Calvaire.
O^{bis} Bagnolet (Mairie)-Pont-Neuf.
R. Clichy (Pl. Lecomte) par Bd. Jean-Jaurès-Hôtel-de-Ville.
R^{bis} Clichy (Mairie) par Bd de Lorraine-Hôtel-de-Ville.
S. Courbevoie (Gare de Bécon)-Porte de Champerret-Place de la Contrescarpe.
U. Levallois (Place de Villiers)-Porte de Champerret-Gobelins.
AZ. Neuilly (par l'Av. de Neuilly), Porte de Neuilly-Place Daumesnil.
BA. Vincennes (Mairie)-Porte de Vincennes-Opéra (Rue Taitbout).
BD. Bois-Colombes (Marché)-Porte de Champerret-Église St-Médard 5e.
BG. Montreuil (Mairie)-Porte de Bagnolet-Opéra (rue du 4-Septembre).
BH. Pantin (Rue Courtois)-Porte Chaumont-Les Halles.
BL. Montreuil (Place Carnot)-Porte de Montreuil-Opéra.
BM. Bagnolet (Floréal)-Opéra.
BN. Les Lilas (Paul de Kock)-République.
EA/EN. Dugny-Le Bourget Drancy-Noisy.
EB. Parc St-Maur (Gare)-Place de la Pie.
EC. Parc St-Maur (Gare)-Pont de Chennevières.
ED. Villetaneuse (Mairie)-La Courneuve (4 routes).

EF. Gennevilliers (Les Grésillons)-Saint-Denis (Mutualité).
EG. Porte de Neuilly-Levallois (Mairie).
EH. Vitry (Gare)-Vitry (Place Cavé).
EI. Charenton (Gare)-Charentonneau (Place Delalain).
EJ. Petit-Clamart-Clamart (Mairie).
EK. Pantin (R. Courtois)-Porte de la Villette.
EL. Champigny (Gare)-Cœuilly.
EM. St-Germain-le-Pecq-Chatou-Rueil (Ville).
EO. Pierrefitte-Porte de la Villette.
EP. Nanterre (Gare)-Puteaux (Mairie).
EQ. Malabry-L'Hay-les-Roses-Place d'Italie.
ER. Montreuil (Mairie)-Porte de Vincennes.
ES. Boulogne-Carrefour-Sèvres-Galliéni-Porte de Saint-Cloud.
ET. Créteil (Grande Rue)-St-Maur (Gare).
EU. Clamart (Mairie)-Porte de St-Cloud.
EV. Port-Marly-Marly-le-Roi.
EW. Bois-Colombes-Gare de Nanterre.
EX. Pte de Versailles-Lyc. Michelet-Pte de Versailles.
EY. Fresnes-Fontenay-aux-Roses.
EZ. Argenteuil (Pl. du 11 Novembre)-Colombes (Pl. Galilée).
FA. Alfortville (Pl. du Pt-Pont)-Alfortville (Mairie).
FB. St-Ouen (Mairie)-Aubervilliers (Mairie).
FC. Villejuif-Belle-Épine.
49 La Courneuve-Gare du Nord.
SS. Orly-Choisy-le-Roi (Gare).

NOMENCLATURE DES LIGNES DE TRAMWAYS

1 Versailles-Louvre.
2 Saint-Cloud-Louvre.
3 Vincennes (Château)-St-Mandé-Louvre.
4 Montreuil (7 Chemins)-Nation-Bastille-Louvre.
6 A Vincennes (Chât.)-Porte de Vincennes-Louvre.
6 B Bry-s.-Marne-Nogent-s.-Marne-Porte de Vincennes-République.
9 St-Denis (Église Neuve)-La Chapelle-Jardin des Plantes.
10 St-Ouen (Mairie)-Porte de Clignancourt-Bastille.
11 A Cimetière de St-Ouen-Place de la Nation-Mairie de St-Mandé.
11 B Pierrefitte-République.
13 A Créteil-Charenton-Louvre.
13 B Adamville-Saint-Maur-Charenton-Louvre.
16 Boulogne-Auteuil-Madeleine.
18 St-Cloud-Porte de St-Cloud-St-Sulpice.
21 A Le Raincy-Opéra.
21 B Pavillons-sous-Bois-Opéra.
21 C Noisy-le-Sec-Opéra.
21 D Bobigny-Opéra.
22 Montreuil-(Mairie)-Nation-République-Louvre.
23 Auteuil (Gare)-Les Moulineaux-Pte-Versailles.
24 Maisons-Alfort-Charenton (Écoles)-Place de la République.
25 St-Cloud-Auteuil-St-Sulpice.
29 A Pantin-Gare Montparnasse.
29 B Pré-St-Gervais-Gare Montparnasse.
32 Auteuil (Gare)-Porte de Versailles.
34 Asnières (Pce Voltaire)-Gare d'Austerlitz.
35 Courbevoie (Pont de la Jatte)-Madeleine.
36 Levallois (Quai Michelet)-Place-Pereire.
37 Neuilly (St-James)-Madeleine.
38 Puteaux (Marché)-Porte Maillot.

39 Gennevilliers-Madeleine.
40 Argenteuil-Porte de Clichy-Place de Clichy.
41 La Garenne (Charlebourg) - Porte de Neuilly-Madeleine.
42 St-Denis (Barrage)-Madeleine.
43 Courbevoie (Pt-de-Neuilly)-Gare Montparnasse.
44 St-Cloud-Val d'Or-Suresnes-Porte Maillot.
45 Asnières (Carr. des Bourguignons)-Madeleine.
47 Kremlin-Bicêtre-Pte d'Italic-Pte la Chapelle.
48 St-Denis (Barrage)-Opéra.
49 La Courneuve-Aubervilliers (Mrie)-Gare Nord.
50 Aubervilliers (Mairie)-Pce de la République.
51 Drancy (Écoles)-Place de la République.
52 Le Bourget (Port Aérien)-Aubervilliers-Opéra.
53 St-Denis (Mairie)-Place de la République.
54 Enghien-St-Denis-St-Ouen-Trinité.
58 St-Germain-Bougival-Porte de Neuilly.

61 Argenteuil-Bezons.
62 Maisons-Laffitte-Pte de Neuilly (par le Rond-Point de la Défense).
62 bis La Garenne (Charlebourg)-Porte de Neuilly.
63 Bezons (Grand Cerf)-Porte Champerret.
64 Argenteuil-Porte Champerret.
65 Pierreffitte-St-Denis (Ég. Neuve)-Pte Clignancourt.
66 Colombes (Gare)-Porte de Clignancourt.
69 Montmorency-Enghien.
70 St-Denis (Pte Paris)-Aubervilliers (Mairie)-Porte de la Villette.
71 La Courneuve-Aubervilliers-Porte de la Villette.
72 Le Bourget (Port Aérien)-Porte de la Villette.
73 St-Ouen (Mairie)-Porte de Neuilly.
75 St-Cloud-Asnières (Place Voltaire).
76 La Garenne (Charlebourg)-Porte de Neuilly.
77 Asnières (Place Voltaire)-St-Denis (Ég. Neuve).

79 Stains-St-Denis (Barrage).
80 Bagneux (Cimetière Parisien)-Porte d'Orléans.
81 Maisons-Alfort-Charenton-Bastille.
82 Vitry (Gare)-Ivry-Châtelet.
83 Thiais-Choisy-le-Roi-Châtelet.
84 Petit-Ivry-Porte d'Ivry-Les Halles.
85 Villejuif (Asile)-Châtelet.
86 Fontenay-aux-Roses-Châtillon-Châtelet.
87 Malakoff (rue des Clozeaux)-Halles.
88 Pont d'Antony-Porte d'Orléans.
89 Clamart-Hôtel de Ville.
90 Clamart (Mairie)-Clamart (Gare).
93 Cachan-Arcueil-Châtelet.
94 Clamart (Fourche)-Malakoff (rues Clozeaux).
95 A Pavillons-sous-Bois (Gargan)-République.
95 B Montreuil (La Boissière)-République.
98 Montreuil (7 Chemins)-République.
101 Romainville-Bagnolet-Bastille-Htel-Châtelet.
103 Bonneuil-République.

105 Vitry (Église)-Gare d'Austerl.
107 Aubervilliers (Mairie)-Montre (Mairie).
108 Champigny (Ville)-Porte de Vcennes.
109 La Varenne (g)-Champigny (Pte Vincennes.
110 A La Varenne (Gare)-Porte de Vcennes.
110 B Bonneuil-Porte de Vincennes.
112 Montfermeil-Le Raincy.
113 Gournay-Porte de Vincennes.
114 La Maltournée-Porte de Vincnes-Châtelet.
115 Montreuil-Porte de Vcennes.
116 La Maltournée-Rosny-sous-B.
118 Villemomble-République.
119 Champigny-Nogent-Porte de Vcennes.
120 Noisy-le-Grand-Porte de Vincs.
121 Villemomble (Gare de Gagny)-Vincennes.

122 Fontenay-sous-Bois-Porte de Vincennes.
125 Pte de Vincennes-Pte d'Orléans (extra-muros).
126 Pte d'Orléans-Pte St-Cloud (extra-muros).
127 Fontenay-aux-Roses-Châtillon-St-Germain-des-Prés.
128 Sceaux-Porte d'Orléans.

TRACTION VAPEUR

Arpajon-Montlhéry-Porte d'Orléans.
Embranchement : Montlhéry-Marcoussis.

RÉSEAU des CHEMINS de FER de GRANDE BANLIEUE

Réseau Nord

1° Saint-Germain-Poissy.
2° Poissy-Pontoise.
3° Pontoise-Les Mureaux.
4° Saint-Germain-Les Mureaux.
5° Versailles-Maule-Les Mureaux.
6° Les Mureaux-Magny-en-Vexin.

Réseau Sud

1° Arpajon-Étampes.
2° Étampes-Maisse.
3° Étampes-La Ferté-Alais.
4° Maisse-Milly-Corbeil.

Renault PR180, 4645, passing the Louvre on 28th August 1989. *(Julian Osborne)*